Raising Princes to be Kings: A Black Single Mother's Guide to Raising Her Black Son.

The End Started With a Beginning...

In writing my final chapter – I realized that after speaking to so many black mothers – I have come to understand that there are many levels of black single motherhood...

The Traditional Single Black Mother – It's just her and her children, there are no men living in her home, single income home. Family and support systems are sparse.

The Married Black Single Mother – Yes, She is married right up to the second knuckle in carats & begets. Husband/Dad is always working several jobs and has a side hustle as well. Married Black Single Mother has been ascribed to taking care of the kids; after all, hubby is making the cheese. The thing to keep in mind here is society sees this black mother alone and immediately labels her as the 'traditional black single mother.' This labeling of her and her children comes with negative stigmas and assumptions. The working spouse/father is viewed as the absentee father.

The Part-Time Black Single Mother- Yes, she exists; she has custody of her black son for six months of the year. Imagine how challenging it is for her to assert any kind of authority anywhere. **The Other Part-Time Black Single Mother** is doing her mother responsibilities in-between boyfriends. A new dating prospect cannot know right away that she has kids. One minute this mother is around, the next minute she is gone with the new boyfriend; leaving the black son in the care of whomever. Imagine the instability in this young child's mind and life.

The Long Term Relationship Single Black Mother – She is with the father of her son, but they are not married. This aspect of her relationship could impact her black son in society. The father really has to be a strong, constant presence in the black son's life.

If any of these women describe you and your black son – please read this book and write in the margins – take ownership of the contents of this book and be ready to change –Be ready to raise your black son into a king.

THE BLACK FAMILY PLEDGE

BECAUSE we have forgotten our ancestors, our children no longer give us honor. BECAUSE we have lost the path our ancestors cleared kneeling in perilous undergrowth, our children cannot find their way. BECAUSE we have banished the God of our ancestors, our children cannot pray. BECAUSE the old wails of our ancestors have faded beyond our hearing, our children cannot hear us crying. BECAUSE we have abandoned our wisdom of mothering and fathering, our befuddled children give birth to children they neither want nor understand. BECAUSE we have forgotten how to love, the adversary is within our gates, an holds us up to the mirror of the world shouting, "Regard the loveless" Therefore we pledge to bind ourselves to one another, to embrace our lowliest, to keep company with our loneliest, to educate our illiterate, to feed our starving, to clothe our ragged, to do all good things, knowing that we are more than keepers of our brothers and sisters. We ARE our brothers and sisters. IN HONOR of those who toiled and implored God with golden tongues, and in gratitude to the same God who brought us out of hopeless desolation, we make this pledge.
Written by Maya Angelou.

Introduction

This book not to judge or berate black single mothers; I believe black Moms have done a hell of a job without societal support or respect. I have noticed in my travels that many black men in the world today are troubled and unproductive with very little sound motivation (for the most part). Many young men have difficulty with themselves and in relationships. In this age of advanced technology, why are black men in prisons, school dropouts, in poor relationships, are absentee fathers and non-productive contributors to economic growth and society?

This book will explore how history on black culture has impacted black motherhood, relationships and productivity. I wrote this book to uplift black single mothers; so that they may share the joy and power of successful parenting, the power of the womb, a sense of accomplishment and, contributing to the development of a productive black man who is capable and able to be himself; a father, lover and leader.

To be a black single mom of a son requires strength, courage, faith, determination, organization and respect of self. It is a tough undertaking. I can truly understand the frustration and anger of many black activists. My remedy: Get Involved! Stop blaming! It is my hope that this book and its aftermath will result in a positive contribution that will help many single black moms and their sons. I want to see victory and joy in black parenting – I want to see our black youth embrace their heritage; possess a fear of God and become productive citizens who are not incarcerated, undereducated and drug addicted due to low self esteem.

Our culture – our ancestors in Africa *embraced* pregnancy, childbirth, breast-feeding and motherhood. Children were valued. Today in America, our children are abused, abandoned, unhealthy and given sub-par education. Our most treasured investment – our children need to be valued and validated. Our black sons need to embrace their princedom and prepare to be kings – as their ancestors were and our spirits are today.

Until the United States places the value/respect of pregnancy into the mainstream by supporting natural childbirth, support stronger maternity benefits, employer childcare locations and breastfeeding locations – the entire scope of motherhood will continue to be treated as a disease. Until more stringent laws are in place to protect children from abuse and neglect our children will not be ready or able to inherit the future. Our children need to be valued in education, health, protection and family. Our children need our presence, values, manners and spiritual growth. Currently, there are violent crimes committed against children along with neglect, lack of health insurance, lack of boundaries/guidance and low standards/expectations.

We, the parents have labeled our children "Generation X" and pushed them into adulthood way before they are ready. Today our children are overweight, have mental health issues, do poorly in schools with a predictable future of low paying jobs, are in violent relationships, teen pregnancy, and become a burden on society when these children – our future investments should be an asset. We are now so concerned with being green – to save our earth. Our children have to be saved.

The most popular and frequent response I receive from people when I told them what my book is about: "You should write something for these grown black men who are not doing the right thing as fathers!" That reaction is fine – but I can't do anything with grown men. It is my hope that I can reach black baby boys through their moms who take a chance and read my book or attend my seminar. By starting with black men as baby boys – hopefully a new pattern of behavior will emerge and be a chain breaker for what we know now. I look forward to a new day when children will be treasured and our elderly will be revered.

In no way is my book to be a substitution for a dedicated clinical book/manual on pregnancy such as "What to Expect When You Are Expecting." This book is merely an enhancement to anything clinically related to pregnancy that you are reading. It is my hope that my book will collaborate with an infusion of diversity and likeness that will motivate!

I could not be the person I am today if it were not for God's continued presence in my life, the sacrifice of my ancestors and my parents Solomon Jr. and Zenobia Bolds. These two people dedicated their lives to my every need. I was loved by these two people and I will never forget that love. My father taught me the values of the importance of family; my mother taught me devotion and holding God as the highest power.

Together, my parents were a formidable team of "Buzz and Junior." They worked shoulder to shoulder and they lived a life of imperfections that was both realistic and humbling. My father gave the best hugs, my mother is the best secret keeper and side kick a girl can have! My mother is my Honey Pot!

To the women in my life, those who have come and gone or stayed your presence in my life changed me. There were so many clouds in my life, you all of you are my rainbows that I cherish and will never forget: Tena Garrett, Marie Bolds, Maureen Guinan, Nurit Harris, Maureen Mullarkey-Schwartz, Frances Snyder, Carmen McGill, Geri Pozzi-Galluzzi, Ethel Paxton, Pat Vinson, Deborah Reeves-Duncan, Jackie Goffe-McNish,

Marilyn Green, CSW, Terri L. Cade, Marilynn Vetrano, Shirley Riley, Oprah Winfrey and Cathedral High School Class of 1982.

Of course there have been men in my life – Men who have accepted me for who I am and have cheered me forward with my dreams. Some of these men I have worked shoulder to shoulder with; others have made a contribution to my life that I will never forget: Richard Garrett, Stu Stein, Lateef Islam, Russell Simmons, Everett Patterson Jr., Ron Nelson, Dr. Peter Gergley and Baballow Conrad Mague.

Thank you to my son Jordan – My little sprout that has grown to be a tree that gives me shade and breeze; you are my brightest and most beautiful rainbow in so many clouds! Thank you for trusting me all these years and showing me the woman I was meant to be. You have always accepted me the way I am: nurturer, warrior, daughter, mother, and black woman! I love you so very much. I could have never written this book if I did not have you in my life! I enjoy witnessing your transition from a prince to a king!

Last but not least – this book is to all the students of the Class of 2008 Poughkeepsie High School, Poughkeepsie, NY. You all allowed me to be your champion and I thank you. I cannot tell you how important your shout-outs, hugs, shy waves and hellos mean to me whenever you see me, you greet me and I am so touched by your kindness. I will forever be "Ms. Jordan's Mom" to you. All of you have my prayers of safety, protection and prosperity by God for you.

To Roary, you get me up on time every time.

To Lucky, you are the true Mama of the house.

To my 'Shero' Dr. Donda West and my Hero Solomon Bolds Jr.: I now hold the baton you have passed onto me – I am going to run with it for as long as I can.

Table of Contents

4. Television, Video Games and Learning.

5. Your Black Son in School.

6. Your Special Needs Black Son.

Chapter Six –Nutrition and Neuro Development   Page 147

 1. A Good Diet = Healthy Baby = Strong King

2. Baby Boy Needs Stimulation!

3. Do's and Don'ts.

4. Mama's Nutrition & Stimulation – Yes You Can!

5. Letting Go of thePast.

Chapter Seven – Adolescence   Page 165

1. Be a Leader – Not a Follower.

2. Show You Care – Listen.

3. Mental Health and the Black Son.

 4. The Angry Black Son.

5. Mentoring.

6. Sex Talk.

7. Sexual Preference and the Black Son.

8. Keep Your Sexuality Separate from Your Son's Sexuality.

9. Being a Pal Sometimes– ALWAYS A Mom!!!

10. Have your Black Son's Back!

11. The Death Talk.

<u>*****All work NOT by Ms. Bolds is cited on the page used.**</u>

Phenomenal Woman

Pretty women wonder where my secret lies. I'm not cute or built to suit a fashion model's size But when I start to tell them, They think I'm telling lies. I say, It's in the reach of my arms The span of my hips, The stride of my step, The curl of my lips. I'm a woman Phenomenally. Phenomenal woman, That's me. I walk into a room Just as cool as you please, And to a man, The fellows stand or Fall down on their knees. Then they swarm around me, A hive of honey bees. I say, It's the fire in my eyes, And the flash of my teeth, The swing in my waist, And the joy in my feet. I'm a woman Phenomenally. Phenomenal woman, That's me. Men themselves have wondered What they see in me. They try so much But they can't touch My inner mystery. When I try to show them They say they still can't see. I say, It's in the arch of my back, The sun of my smile, The ride of my breasts, The grace of my style. I'm a woman Phenomenally. Phenomenal woman, That's me. Now you understand Just why my head's not bowed. I don't shout or jump about Or have to talk real loud. When you see me passing It ought to make you proud. I say, It's in the click of my heels, The bend of my hair, the palm of my hand, The need of my care, 'Cause I'm a woman Phenomenally. Phenomenal woman, That's me.

Maya Angelou*

*Angleou, Maya. "Phenomenal Woman". Random House, 1995.

Chapter One

The Future Mother: Pre-conceptual Health & Pregnancy

The most empowering attribute of a woman is motherhood. Humanity depends upon a woman's ability to conceive, carry and nurture a child. Pre-conceptual health care is essential for women from a very young age through menopause. Pre-conceptual health education and support addresses female health in a holistic approach with the focus being reproductive health care.

Adolescent females whom receive pre-conceptual training and support have a stronger self-esteem, contraceptive practices, awareness of the dangers of drug use, domestic violence and an understanding that a female's health *before* she becomes pregnant is just as vital as the nine months of OB care. Human eggs are not only vulnerable to genetics, but to the environment: drugs, alcohol, poor self care, violence and stress all contribute to the unborn child being susceptible to being born with a genetic defect, deficiency or disability.

Our children are the best natural resource on the planet. They are the most solid investment we can ever make. It is imperative that the intrinsic value of children and youth be embraced from the government to every person in every community.

As the result of the onset of puberty, young females will benefit from pre-conceptual health education and support; thus humanity will thrive with healthy babies. This education program can be introduced and maintained in schools, community centers and churches. The fact does remain: black women are more susceptible to stressful upbringing and adult life; their children inherit this stress. With the epidemic of HIV/Aids, Hepatitis C and Sexual Transmitted Infections (STI) – communities have to support young females in order to see a procreation of healthy black people. Pre-conceptual health education empowers young females about their sexuality and promotes responsible thought. **A woman is as powerful if she understands her sexuality and controls it – sex does not control her.**

Pre conceptual health care taught early to young girls will promote better behaviors and awareness through education and empowerment that education bring about in individuals. Imagine how much money the government will save by implementing this education nationwide. Remember the United States Surgeon General Jocelyn Elders appointment during the Clinton Administration? Dr. Elders had to step down from her appointment because she strongly promoted and advised teens to use condoms, not abstinence and for condoms to be available in schools. America still refuses to be transparent about sex to our youth. Dove has a new self esteem campaign out for girls – for empowerment and yet the issue of sex still is carefully avoided. Women need to have the history of their gender taught to them as well as the science of their bodies as well. In my undergrad studies, I took a life changing class of Women's History taught by Dr. George Stevens.

Dr. Stevens is a white male who sat in a room filled with women twice a week and blew our minds on the history of women in America. If the history of white women in America is not mainstream—then you can imagine how obscure the history of women of color is in America. Black young women have to see and know of Black History of Women, the introduction of these strong, successful women is the foundation of young, feminine self-esteem.

Teens are having sex – and socioeconomics has nothing to do with it. Rich and poor teens are doing it, black and white. Here are some facts: The average age of first intercourse in 16.9 for boys and 17.4 for girls according to the Alan Guttmacher Institute*. There are about 750,000 pregnancies per year with one third of those pregnancies being aborted and the remaining two thirds going to full term. The Centers for disease Control reports that teen moms are less likely to finish high school and are more likely to remain single parents. STI/STD's are also on the rise in teens with most going undetected due to lack of education/awareness. Teens need to be encouraged to seek sex education via the internet, libraries or Planned Parenthood, go with a friend. I give young women who I knew were going off to college a copy of "Our Bodies – Ourselves." The cost of preventative intervention is always cheaper than reactive crisis.

*Kliff, Sarah. Newsweek Web Exclusive: "Teen Pregnancy, Hollywood Style." Retrieved July 27, 2008. www.newsweek.com/id/148437.

Parenting By Choice Not By Chance!

You had sex – now you are pregnant. Many women have not practiced pre-conceptual health, as mentioned above. Taking folic acid, exercising, watching drug and alcohol intake and having possession of family history is vital in preparation for mother hood. Don't panic – now is the time to get an Obstetrician (OB) immediately – take full advantage of your state's prenatal health programs, WIC and read up on your condition. Pregnancy is not a disease – as the medical profession is treating it as. Pregnancy is a natural condition that your body is made to handle.

Another support is to have a **mentor** during your pregnancy (Mama Mentor). This mentor that you choose should be accessible, have experience as a mother (medical background is also helpful) this person must be level headed, easy to talk with, respects confidentiality and utilizes common sense. The black woman is the only woman that can conceive and not really know the actual color her baby will come out as. I have seen black women give birth to white babies! Babies with green or blues eyes and red hair! Anything is possible. This is because of our genealogy – our ancestors are so diverse, our babies represent the rainbow of the world. **Remember**—Once you have agreed to keep this pregnancy, your life as you know it has changed; boundaries, sacrifice, hard work and humility are what is required for success.

Now is the best time to get into the mind set of contributing to your baby's health. Here are a few areas of importance:

* Environment: Your home is harmonious, free of stress – a safe place that you can relax rest and rejuvenate. You will also want this kind of environment for you and your baby to live in.

* Diet: You need to eat for TWO. Cravings are fine and normal. Your diet should be healthy – a prenatal vitamin is also very helpful. Follow your OB/Midwife's guidance and also a consultation with a nutritionist is also very helpful.

* Exercise: Walking, gentle stretches, swimming and yoga are all very important during pregnancy to help

your body metabolize and produce endorphins and help with your labor.

    * Superstitions: Well, you have probably heard quite a few of them! As your belly grows – look out – you will hear more!

    * Talk with your OB/Midwife about your delivery options very carefully. Having a baby is a natural process that your body was built for. Caesarian Section is major surgery and the recuperation/recovery time is longer and you are more prone to post surgical complications. **Make sure you have thoroughly discussed all options with your medical provider before signing consent!**

    Having a C-Section is in no way down playing your ability to being a mother. Many women feel inadequate because they had to have a section when the hope was to have a natural birth. At the same time – please do not use a c-section to 'schedule' what is a natural process, giving birth.

    The United States has seen an increase in c-section deliveries and the media also highlights celebrities who do. Having a c-section for a medically necessary reason is justified, having a c-section because you don't want to go into labor or want to have a pretty baby, or have a tummy tuck, or because you heard that your vaginal muscles with stretch out – whatever the reason, **having a c-section is a method of last resort to save you and your baby.**

It's all in the Birth!

Nine Months of eating right, sleeping and staying drug free. Maintaining a positive attitude and atmosphere and now you are up to the time of giving birth. As I said, giving birth is a very natural process that your body is equipped to do. You have your birth plan and you are as ready as you are going to be. Labor is quite unpredictable and no two women are alike; no two pregnancies are alike. The best, uneventful pregnancy could have labor complications, your baby may come earlier than his due date. The skill of your Obstetrician, the facility you are utilizing to give birth at as well as the staff is vital now.

There has been an increase of children with ADD/ADHD. This may be the result of increased awareness and data to help identify what was once virtually unrecognizable. Think for a minute if you are very healthy and as far as you know, there is no ADD/ADHD in the family. You gave birth to your son and a few years later he has this diagnosis. How? It very well may be in the birth process and the method taken and the drugs given. It is necessary for the medical field in the area of **Obstetrics and Perinatology** to do further research, investigations and identify the increase of babies being born with ADD/ADHD in the past 20 years.

There has also been an increase of gestational diabetic pregnancies resulting in the birth of very large babies. Now the medical profession has tons of data; only a good practitioner utilizes that data to benefit their patients. There are studies that verify that if the pregnant mom has her gestational diabetes managed very well and her blood sugars are under close monitoring and supported by good diet and even and insulin pump, the result is the birth of a baby at a healthy weight. This action will reduce the possibility of this baby becoming an obese individual as an adult and a possible diabetic as well.

Why do I mention these two examples? Well in my travels in medical education it has come to my attention that there is medical data to support the above statements that would reduce both ADHD and overweight children with future risk of becoming diabetics themselves. How is it then that this knowledge is not mainstream and practiced in a proactive attitude? It may be due to the all mighty dollar. In the future, I would strongly support research on diabetic pregnancies and obese adults as well as the connection between ADD/ADHD and the birthing techniques/treatments used.

As with so many institutions in America money and profit dominate. It is lucrative to keep people in a state of dependency on the medical profession because someone is making a profit of the drug, testing, research, treatment modality – someone is making a profit off of another person's diagnosis. Having healthy babies on a universal level of health should be paramount, but it is not. This same model applies in education as well as the judicial system; run them like a business for a profit and only provide a certain level of success to maintain the dependency to keep the profit viable. This is just pure evil, and a no-win situation all around.

Naming Your Son

I have encountered some outrageous names: Supreme, Lord, Your Majesty, ESPN, Etc. Phonetic miss-spellings are also out (boyz, etc). My belief is to name your son so that when his name is seen on an application, his name will not be a dead giveaway to his ethnicity or socioeconomic status. A simple yet beautiful name such as my son's name Jordan – has immediately associated with Michael Jordan – not the Jordan River a place of miracles and commitment as I was thinking when I named my son.

Yes, the name of your son shapes his destiny. Historically, the man, the head of household gave his wife and children his last name for a few reasons: Protection, and inventory of his own wealth, the more children, the more workers for the farm and such. Can the father of your child provide protection if you give your baby his last name? Will the father of your baby share his wealth with his child? All of this must be considered. A name is the passing of heritage and traditions. Do you have access to your baby's father's heritage and traditions? A name identifies and historically a name is associated with power and privilege. It is important for you to understand this.

Your son should not be named after a material possession such as a car, liquor or favorite food. Stick with the Bible, African History or honor an ancestor. REALLY think about naming your son after his father - make sure you really want to do this. I have heard of a superstition that naming your son after a person who had a hard life - your son will have a hard life as well. Ask someone in your family about this one! Your pregnancy is a time of celebration of a miracle. Your pregnancy is an event that is to inspire and motivate you to be the best person and mother you can be.

Remember - your uterus is powerful; your son is not to be a bargaining chip or a way to hold onto a man. Your son is the tree that will give you shade and protection and yield the fruit of laughter and joyful pride of accomplishments.

Baby Mama – NO DRAMA!!!

Stress For the Black Woman - From the Womb to the Tomb!

You have made a choice to keep this pregnancy – now you find yourself a black single mother of a son. This role and responsibility is *serious*. This is no time to be a victim or expect a hand out. **You** are responsible for the health, safety and development of this male child. Start by having a healthy pregnancy that is drug, cigarette and violence free. Have a pregnancy that has laughter, maturity and a future with plans. A goal without a plan is just an idea! Plans are long term actions and goals – Successful blacks are those who see themselves in long term planning and not just living day-to-day. Day-to-day living worked on the plantation; not in today's society.

Motherhood can be a wonderful self-esteem builder. Affirm that you will be successful as a mother, put work and effort into motherhood and your son. Refer to the Contracts Chapter and take the oath! As I will discuss further in this book – black females are regarded in society as the lowest forms. We are according to other races irresponsible, promiscuous, loud, and uncultured. I read an interesting article written by Sophia Nelson, dated July 20, 2008. Ms Nelson writes: "We've watched with a mixture of pride and trepidation as the wife of the first serious African American presidential contender has weathered recent campaign travails – being called unpatriotic for a single offhand remark, dubbed a black radical because of

something she wrote more than 20 years ago and
plastered with the crowning stereotype 'angry black
woman.'" *

*Nelson, Sophia, A. "Black. Female. Accomplished. Attacked. Washington Post July 20,
2008 Electronic Retrieval September 11, 2008. www.washingtonpost.com/wp-
dyn/content/article/2008/0718/AR2008071802557_pf.html.

The article goes on to describe how Mrs. Obama
had to undergo a politically mandated makeover to soften
her image and make her more 'acceptable' to mainstream
America. I have been called "Angry black woman" so many
times. I know that if I were blond hair and blue eyes, I
would be declared brilliant with my Master's Degree. This
statement does have correlation in the validity of why so
many black women make themselves appear as white
featured as possible – for acceptance. This is a malformed
action of assimilation.

Serena Williams also brilliantly describes this
phenomenon on HBO's "The Black List" As a professional
tennis player of great distinction, Ms. Williams' description
of her plays and her actions are much harsher than her
white peers who have been involved in a wide range of
scandals from drugs, sex, etc. Oprah Winfrey can't fart

without the tabloids making a negative story. I can remember one of the tabloids doing a huge 'expose' on Ms. Winfrey's feet. All of the humanitarian deeds Ms. Winfrey have done and the media focuses on her feet... Ms. Winfrey is one of the top media earners in history – who cares if she has an issue with her feet that is probably genetically inherited. Ms. Brooke Shields had a similar issue and yes, the media was very gentle in describing Ms. Shields' 'foot augmentation...'

Where did this image originate from? Slavery. Since slavery, black women had to be strong: defending themselves, leading the family, handling their business. There was little time to learn to be soft, passive and ultra feminine. Black women are the originators of multitasking. Black women had to do this in order to survive. Remember, slavery lasted for 400 years. Black women have perfected the skill of multitasking and surviving. This lack of appreciation from society for this survival skill has resulted in the negative regard and descriptions for the black woman. Also, the black man has also picked up on this regard and descriptions of their women, their queens. Rare is the black man who understands and does not view black women this way.

As a black single parent, I have been called every negative description in the book. It is a rare encounter where my survival skills and strengths are praised. Oprah Winfrey, Serena Williams and Michelle Obama are not the only beacons of light for black women, there are some locally where you are. Find them, praise them and get them in your support circle. These women are priceless in their wisdom and dedication to up holding our people. These women you choose to be in your support circle will most likely support you as well.

I Ain't Sayin' She's a Gold-Digger...

Kayne West's lyrics stay in my head since I first heard the song. Black single mothers can easily find themselves in **Family Court** for child support – visitation, support and custody establishment. This is a very serious matter: black single moms should always establish custody of their sons. By establishing yourself as the sole custodial parent gives you power and authority over many legal things such as insurance policies, scenarios requiring contracts and many more. I can speak from both personal and professional experiences in the interactions in Family Court. I am going to keep it real...

What about his mental history? How was he raised? Now that If he wasn't shit before – what makes you think he has changed now that you had a baby for him? He (the father) is not going to change and you can't fix him either – my suggestion: Do like the animals on the nature shows - locate the best male to procreate with. How well do you know this man? Did you meet him in the dark at a party? Get a better look in the bright of day. **<u>Do you know your baby's father?</u>**

The most dynamic time throughout my pregnancy was signing the paper stating I am my son's parent and I am responsible for him before taking him home. Family Court is not for women. The judges and lawyers are predominately men and a few horrible cases of neglectful mothers painted lasting stigmas for all mothers. You cannot obtain Public Assistance unless you identify your baby's daddy. The courts will help you find him so the State won't have to take the brunt of financial responsibility for your son – the daddy pays. It really looks like Mom is hounding the absentee dad – but if Mom wants state benefits – even medical coverage – this is what she must go through to get it. This request could place that mom in physical harm from the absentee father.

Let's Go Back in the Day... *Historically, women were solely responsible for motherhood and child rearing. Society* *expected women to produce children to man farms and armies. When something is wrong with a child – it is immediately assumed that the mother is at fault. This ideology has carried into today's Family Court and for black mothers Family Court is especially harsh and so reminiscent of slavery where black mothers had their babies ripped from their arms. To be a woman in Family Court is harsh enough – to be a black woman in Family Court is virtually fatal.*

A negative stigma against women is that child support goes to the mother and the child does not get the proceeds (Yes, there are a few mothers out there who actually do this and they need to be dealt with). Many fathers believe their child support goes to the mother and therefore they virtually refuse to pay and will even go so far as to take low paying jobs off the books so they don't have to pay. First of all – there is no value to the cost of motherhood. It is such an injustice to the child when the biological father does not contribute financially – this opens up so many other vulnerabilities that will be addressed further in this book.

I think it was Diddy who wanted to 'buy out of fatherhood' - If he really wanted to do that – a condom

nine months before would have given everyone a break!
Let's take this to the next level – have a vasectomy! Most
men would never agree because of pride and male ego:
it's better to produce these children and go through all the
drama – rather than take the necessary precautions. Is
shooting blanks worse than siring children and then
spending years fighting not to support them? Child
support is given to the mother for the child – yes she has
to spend money on shelter, food and clothing. Don't forget
the incidentals as well as the last minute items. Yes, she
has to take care of herself and her son. I am not in support
of any mother who knowingly targets a man who is making
big money and has a baby for him just because of his
earnings. Your child is not your meal ticket.

Remember – YOU PAY THE COST TO BE THE BOSS!!! – For
example: paying for your son's non-covered medical bill of
$ 850.00, the doctor's office require this balance to be
paid up front or within 30 days. You go to Family Court to
get your son's father to pay his share (usually 50%) – the
court then arranges for the father to pay *in installments* of
$20-$40 a week until his share is paid. The irony here is

that YOU (the Mom) paid up front, but the non-custodial parent gets top pay small amounts until the bill is paid. This type of arrangement could put you (Mom) in collections by the medical office if you did not pay upfront or in the given guidelines. Also, the absentee father in some courts is allowed to participate in Family Court via telephone, but YOU must take off from work and be present in court or your case will be dismissed. These situations definitely do appear to be one-sided and the amount of stress intensifies. This kind of stress must be kept away from your son.

I say the same thing for women as well – sex is powerful and pleasurable. A woman should never be denied her right to have at least one child. It is when a woman cannot take care of nor support her own children and the children are neglected is where the injustice lies. For women I say pre-conceptual health and practicing birth control is essential. Birth control is a power phrase and its power is the reason many religions prohibit the practice. Of course in a perfect world sex should be experienced between a husband and wife for procreation – but when that does not happen we are not to judge –

simply practice birth control. **Women, take control – BRING YOUR OWN CONDOMS!!! Don't wait on the man to protect you.**

Family court will step in and tell both parents what will and will not occur. Please understand that the father has rights and in a court of men – the mother will be portrayed as conniving, a Jezebel, irresponsible and vindictive. I have personally been in Family Court and witnessed a roomful of men, denouncing the successful single black female parent (even the ex-husband). The ex-husband could not bring himself to praise the single black mom – his ex-wife and mother of his son for her wonderful job of raising her son. Even with the absentee father's choice **not** to contribute to his son's life (in other words abandoning his son). Family Court could not praise the single black mother for keeping her son jail free, drug free, child free and off to college with a wonderful future ahead of him as a productive citizen. Rarely have I ever witnessed a mother being praised in Family Court of men. No matter how successful the single black mother has been - the recognition is rarely given in Family Court. Praise occurs outside of court.

Possession is nine tenths of the law. The woman has the uterus and is the vessel which carries/holds a fetus for nine months. The woman is in control of the decision to keep or terminate the pregnancy. She has to stand before her God, her conscience and her soul in this decision. This is powerful for women. The man has no say really in keeping or terminating the pregnancy (except in marriage or extreme cases). This is why sex is a responsibility – a huge one. The woman may have her say about keeping the baby, but many times the absentee father feels that since he is no longer in the picture, does not interact with the child at all – he is absconded from any financial responsibility. That man is beholden to those 23 chromosomes he has contributed simply because he put his sperm there.

The woman may have the say – but I have witnessed many times the 'retaliation' in Family Court. The Judicial System is a male dominated one, just like the Medical System. Men make the laws, mostly white men. A woman goes into Family Court and you can guarantee that there is an air of blame in that courtroom and it falls to the women. After witnessing so many family court cases, including my own, I can fully understand why some women don't pursue the absentee parent's contribution. It is a long, frustrating process that is demeaning and accusatory in nature. I say to all women: Hang in there and fight for your black son's entitlement! Your black son is at such a disadvantage if you give up. This financial disadvantage has serious ramifications in your son's future. Your black son needs you to fight for him – have your black son's back on this.

THE 64 MILLION DOLLAR QUESTION...

Do you want your child to have interactions with his father? This is a serious question and I ask because everyone including Family Court immediately believes that it is in the best interest of your son to be with his father. In a traditional nuclear family of father, mother and children yes – this scenario is very good and I grew up having both parents. My parents did not abuse drugs; my home was free of violence. Many black children today do not live this way; their homes have drugs, alcohol and violence present. Family Court is fixated on 'the best interest of the child.' This fixation is actually laws that originated in stigmas and Caucasian values. These beliefs have left many sons exposed to violence, drugs and sex. Many sons who have to juggle between two homes of a split family end up as troubled adults in need of therapy. Why? Because having a shoe in each home has its negative ramifications when the **parents do not put the son's best interest first.**

Parents of split homes will often bad mouth the absentee parent conducts themselves in very inappropriate ways with boy/girl friends in the home where the son is staying and also do many age inappropriate things with the son to win his like and love. These behaviors are selfish and cruel. Exposing son's to sex, bad mouthing and poor discipline/boundaries breeds an adult man who is troubled and who will often have poor relationships.

Sons will do well when both parents put the needs of the son first: no badmouthing, consistency in discipline, have boundaries and communication are both key here. Trust and respect are also required from the parents to one another. Your son will witness these positive actions first hand. **The relationship may have failed between you and your son's father – move on and keep your son as your focus first – not your own feelings.**

Visitation is often the crux of many issues: the absentee parent will keep visits initially with his son and then drop off until contact is non-existent. This is so very harmful to your son as these actions erodes trust, creates feelings of abandonment and places such a strain on the present parent – (the Mom) who the son will lash out at in his disappointment and misdirected anger. If it is your weekend to have your son – don't buy him outlandish things to buy his affection. Keep moderation in mind and put that extra money away for your son's education.

Your son needs structure, discipline and boundaries. Arguing in front of your son, you and your boy/girlfriend making out or having sex in front of your son and not providing structure are all the wrongs that will mentally and physically affect your son as he grows into a man. I have witnessed professionally the adverse side of Family Court with regards to visitation, support and custody. Many black sons grow up needing therapy as adults because of what they were exposed to during visitation with the non-custodial parent. (Not all non-custodial parents are like this but many are.)

The custodial parent is totally unaware because the son won't speak of what he was exposed to – only in rare cases. The son is too terrified to speak: to do so may make Mom and Dad fight again or worse – make Dad leave for good.

Black single mothers have to make the choice of financial support and the extra responsibilities that come along with it – as explained above. If your son's father is unstable mentally, transient in home and jobs, takes drugs or lives a lifestyle that places your son in harm's way – is it worth the few dollars a month you get in support? Can you financially raise your son yourself? And provide healthcare? If so – think carefully.

The point I am trying to make is about *safety.* Just how safe will your son be with visitation by his father? In an longitudinal, long term review – will your son grow up to be a positive, strong man because of this interaction, or will he grow up with disappointments, abandonment, trust issues and anger? You really have to think this over very carefully! As I have stated before – once you decide to keep the pregnancy, (your baby) you are making a very long commitment that will demand sacrifice, patience, dedication and humility BY YOU – NOT THE WORLD.

Please do not tell your son he does not have a father – that is physically impossible. Of course your son has a father. If and when your son should ask – let the truth – although sometimes painful prevail. "Yes, you do have a father but your father and I could not get along and I made the choice to keep you."

This Baby is a Human Being – Not an Accessory...

I have seen everything outside of tattooing the infant son and if that were legal I am sure some mother out there would try it. Your son is *not* an accessory: double ear piercing and designer labeled clothing does not a better baby make! The designer outfits won't get that much wear and tear to get your monies worth. Keep your son's clothes simple and comfortable because he will be pooping and spitting all over that Sean John outfit that cost a small fortune! Ear piercing your son as an infant –

well you just took a choice away from your son now when he is able to make the decision on his own as an adult.

What Was I 'Expecting'?

I waited until this time to ask this question because now you are pretty much invested into motherhood. Expectations can lead to disappointment: which can break down self-esteem and cause depression. Keep your sanity – keep a journal and keep your head and your faith up! Many things can and will occur throughout your pregnancy – some challenging and some great! Having your son is worth it! Interact with your Mama Mentor and your support system. Many things can occur in nine months, you may no longer be with the baby's father; you may be homeless or unemployed. You may have a complicated pregnancy (High Risk). Please seek out your support systems both in the community and personal.

Breastfeeding, Circumcision and Smile!

Yes! You have pushed your son out into this world! You are in awe of that this person made you have all these feelings for nine months! The sonogram did not do justice – you are in love at the first sight of him. It is important to take care of your son's penis – yes I know you have watched him yank on it countless times during the sonogram and you will be pissed on every time you change his diaper – circumcision is important. To have the extra foreskin removed will help your son maintain penile hygiene and avoid penile diseases that are found more frequent in uncircumcised men. Please discuss this with the doctor prior to your discharge from the hospital.

Breastfeeding – the most beneficial gift you can give your son – NO! I will not accept mother's saying how breastfeeding feels like their boyfriend sucking their breasts! This is NOT your boyfriend, this is your SON!!! Breastfeeding is NOT sexual. Breast milk is the perfect source of nutrition for your baby – breast milk builds immunity and helps in bonding with your baby. Breast milk is cheaper than formula and your son is less prone to allergies from your breast milk as opposed to formula which your baby can be allergic to.

Breast feeding also helps you stay mindful about maintaining your own nutrition as you are eating to produce the best milk possible. Take advantages of your hospital's lactation support programs – grab that mentor!!! Whip out your breast and feed your baby! If you are out in public – just bring a large shawl and feed your son. Go ahead! Make your son a breast man!

There was nothing like my son's smile when he saw me coming towards him. I am sure he was thinking: "Here comes Lunch!" Don't forget – your nipples will be sore until they toughen up to nursing – **BUT DON'T GIVE UP!!!**

If you did tear your son's delivery or needed an episiotomy, take your time on the toilet, eat food that are natural stool softeners and take your sitz bath! Remember to smile and you will healed in no time! Lastly – Rest Rabbit Rest! Sleep allows the body to heal and rejuvenate. Until your baby boy develops a sound sleep pattern around feedings – You sleep when he sleeps! Stop! Drop! and Snore baby!!!

The Teenage Pregnancy

I would be remiss if I did not include this section in my book. My mother was a teen mother at 16 with my sister back in 1957. It was not the ok to be black, unmarried and pregnant then. I have often spoke to my mother about her life as a teen mom and I love her for her brutal honesty, I will share her responses with you: "I never had any sex education, my mother always told me to keep my drawers on, she never went any further than that." After I have my daughter I went into a shell, I did not talk much and I certainly did not want any kind of a relationship with a man. I was treated like a failure in my family, like I made a huge mistake and I was treated like I had to prove something. This feeling followed me into adulthood with my parents and my family." My mother was sent to New York pregnant so that the small town in South Carolina would not know what happened. She gave her daughter to her older sister to raise.

My mother met my father (also a native of South Carolina) in New York years later. They were married and they had me. For years I knew my sister as my cousin. My mother thought it best to keep the arrangement to avoid the topic of teen pregnancy. My mother got her GED and has been a hard worker all of her life. My mother started out as a clerk in her career and quickly moved up the ladder to management. I think her drive was the result of her teen experience with motherhood. I know my mother experienced a form of emotional trauma being sent away during one of the most frightening times of her life. She had no one to defend her from the scorn of family in New York City where she lived.

For the black teenage mother, the road before you is challenging. You are no Jamie Lynn spears, no Bristol Palin. You do not have the wealth or whiteness that will allow forgiveness. Your pregnancy will be viewed as an act of irresponsibility, whether you used birth control or not. PLEASE GET PRENATAL CARE IMMEDIATELY!!! Don't be in denial; I hate it when a young girl says she did not know she was pregnant. There are too many signs to ignore. Get yourself to safety and get medical attention. It is important to remember that your body is still developing and having a baby stresses your young body. Get the support both mentally and medically that you deserve.

Your pregnancy is a life changing event that is magnified. You have very little education and no job skill to provide for you and your baby. You can still be successful if you focus on being a good mother and building up your life with education, a job skill and a profession that will not have you and your baby dependent upon anyone.

Get it in your mind that the baby's father may not stay with you and the baby. Get it in your mind that this baby needs you and you need to focus on improving your life for you and your baby. Too many times the media distorts the reality – those baby channels about the high risk births and the success stories really don't cover the reality adequately. Having a premature baby escalates the demands on the mother. This special needs baby will grow up to be a special needs child requiring years of intervention to obtain a degree of normalcy and function as an adult.

A baby is not a toy, a fad or a way to get attention. This is a life – take it seriously. Throwing your baby in the garbage or abandoning it in a non-safe environment is cruel as this baby did not ask to be here. There is help out there for you, just step up and take it. You have your whole life ahead of you. If you decide to keep this baby remember the sacrifices you will have to make and the changes you will have to accept. You may be classified as being emancipated from your parents because of this pregnancy and you will have to get benefits on your own and not be eligible to use your parent's health benefits.

Having a baby never, ever holds a man- remember that! YOU are in control of your sexuality, your vagina, your body. Love yourself first and then let love find you. Having a boyfriend and having sex with him does not validate you or complete you. Your body is your temple – take care and take responsibility.

I don't care what you see on television or in the movies – that is the white perspective and that is not real for you, the black woman. If you want real – get yourself a peer teen mom and bond with her – let her share her experiences with you.

Chapter Two

You and Your Son Are Home!

Guess What? Your baby boy did NOT come with any directions! You may be flipping out or be totally terrified – you CAN do this! Make sure you have your Mama Mentor and support systems in place. Get your 6-week post delivery appointment from your OB and **GET SOME BIRTH CONTROL!!!** Keep your son indoors for at least four weeks – that's right, I said four weeks. Only go out for MD visits. Why? In the four weeks you and your son will be getting used to a schedule, bonding time and time to establish a routine for the both of you. The four weeks will give you time to heal and rejuvenate as well as keep your son away from germs, harsh noises and lights.

You know there is always someone who wants to put his/her dirty hands on your son's face!

In four weeks you and your son will be spending time working on feeding, sleeping, cleaning and getting back into the mainstream. Accept help from friends, family and neighbors but also communicate to your support when you and your son need time alone. Stock up on groceries, which save both time and money as well as reduce the possibility of having to run out late at night for something you need. Being with your son on an almost one-on-one basis during these four weeks will allow you to learn about your son: his moods, tone of his cries, his feeding and changing times and sleep patterns.

This time will also allow you to practice diaper changing and how to dress your son in all of those cute outfits you got at your shower! These four weeks may also be challenging if your son is colicky. Talk with your Mama Mentor or an experienced family member for help – DON'T TRY TO MANAGE THIS ALONE!!!! Vibrations are helpful to comfort your colicky son.

Talk with friends and family about a christening or naming ceremony – remember – this event – your son's birth is a celebration. Do take advantage of parenting classes at your local community center, church, hospital or clinic. You will soon be able to recite all of your son's actions to his pediatrician because you will be the mommy expert! At the pediatrician – be open to discuss any observations you have noticed about your son. Also, be open to discuss any kind of depression you may be experiencing after the birth of your son. Remember – community support's sole function is to empower you to be the best mommy you can be!

Sleeping Arrangements

I firmly believe in the 'family bed.' Sorry, but my son did sleep with me (on his back) many of nights. I learned this after breaking a few toes trying to get between the bed and the crib for a twilight feeding (my son is still a night eater to this day). My son still used his crib during the day. I have heard of the unfortunate accidents of babies being smothered in the bed when the mom accidentally rolled onto the sleeping infant. I was one of the lucky ones – my son wasn't ever hurt being in bed with me. I am suggesting that you follow the safest sleep arrangement possible. Keep your son's crib décor simple and with easy to wash materials. Be very careful of all the cute little plush stuff that are in the crib with your son. These plush toys hold dust and can promote allergies as well as be a smothering hazard.

It's Mommy Time!

Ok girl! You made it through the delivery, the sitz baths and he painful stitches, the four weeks at home, the constant flow of family and friends, the twilight feedings, the nipple soreness, the diaper changes, 20 minute naps and now your son is on schedule! You have a reliable and trustworthy sitter (hopefully grandma, god ma or mommy mentor). Your hormones are cooling off and you are starting to look like your old self again. NOW is the time to do you! Groom yourself! Get to the dentist to have your teeth checked post delivery. Get your pedicure! Get rid of that uni-brow! Lotion up after your bath/shower! Take an hour or two and go out with the girls. Make sure you are able to pump your breast milk before you go.

Now is the time to get your journal going again and start interviewing for childcare so when you return to work or school, you will be ahead of the game and have your baby's childcare in place! **Remember** – Your son is relying upon you to be the best person you can be! Focus on your health, safety and ability to provide for your son. Call upon your Mamma Mentor. Additional resources for you are you OB, Midwife or Nurse Practitioner.

Pacifier, Diapers and the Pediatrician

SUCK! SUCK! SUCK! Yeah, I know but...My son loved to nurse – he would latch onto my breast and not eat, he just wanted my nipple in his mouth. I realized early that my son had a very strong sucking reflex and I got him a pacifier. I know I have heard all of the horror stories about using a pacifier and how it causes buck teeth and poor eating habits. I went and researched a very good orthodontic pacifier that fits more to the mouth and does not cause the teeth to shift. To this day my son has never needed braces and he has always had a good appetite. My son never sucked his thumb. My son's pacifier allowed him to self soothe himself and be content.

Diapers – I was insane – I used cloth diapers on my son while we were home and I used disposables when we were out and about. I enjoyed the cloth diapers and my son did not have any diaper rashes or skin irritations. I think I saved a bit of money by using cloth diapers too. You may want to choose as well. My son really did look cute in those diaper wraps and he smelled so sweet in his nappies! Do what is easy and economical for you!

Pediatrician

Your son's doctor is very important part of your success as being a parent. If your pediatrician is not supportive, respectful and through – it's time to make that move to a new one! I could not be the successful single parent I am today if it were not for my son's pediatrician Dr. Peter Gergley, Cold Spring NY. Dr. Gergley's practice is very organized and through; my son and I feel respected as part of a team. The transition for my son from childhood through puberty was also taken into consideration and I slowly found myself moving from the exam room to waiting outside in the waiting area as my son grew into a young man. Dr. Gergley always discussed safety and school relationships with my son and me. When it came time to talk about sexual activity; Dr. Gergley was an excellent source of information and support. My son respects Dr. Gergley so much, he just joked the other day that he will be the only adult patient sitting in Dr. Gergley's waiting room! The race of your son's pediatrician is really not as important as his education and skill as a health care provider. I am glad to have found a male pediatrician, which I think made puberty a bit easier for my son! Make sure your son's pediatrician is a great fit for you and your son!

Support Is More Than a Bra

I could not be the successful single parent I am today if it were not for those near and dear to me they were my support. This small group of people was available to me to talk with, vent to, bounce ideas off of as well as be my cheering squad. Single moms need this so very much. After I gave birth to my son, I was unfortunately misdiagnosed with post partum depression and it was very challenging to recover from. Ever since that dark time in my life I have embraced the care and support from the small circle of those whom I trust. I have to admit along the way, faces and places have changed – I am very grateful to those who have contributed to my success as a Mom and have moved on. 18 years ago post partum depression was not celebrity identified and difficult to discuss. Depression and excessive fatigue needs to be talked about and supported my medical professionals. Please do not ignore this very serious and very frequent occurrence in new moms – keep in mind that blacks are very prone to depression. Motherhood requires a total giving of one's self. It is important that you take care of yourself so you can take care of your son. Nothing is wrong in having a therapist to talk about what you have just gone through, your failed relationship and what you are facing as a single parent. There is no pride in silence – only destruction. Do not take your life for granted, do not risk your son's safety. Post Partum Depression can escalate very quickly into a serious situation!

Chapter Three

Home Sweet Home

Home – A sanctuary for you and your baby

Your womb was once your son's sanctuary; a safe place. Now your home/apartment is his new sanctuary. The home environment is to be a sanctuary for you and your son. Keep your home clean, child safe and violence, drug and alcohol free. Keeping your home clean will reduce germs and illness. A home that is drug free also does not include cigarettes or pharmaceutical medications. Violence free means free from domestic violence from a lover, sibling or other family members. Violence free also means no toy guns, no adult television shows or videos in the form of movies or games. *Please understand that your young son is virtually a human 'sponge' right now. He is soaking up every behavior or words around him and he will repeat and mimic what he sees and hears.*

Your home should be an easy place for you – that's right I said easy. Develop a schedule of chores to do throughout the week so your weekends are free and you are not doing housework all weekend long. By freeing up your time from doing chores – you will have that quality time to spend with your son.

Child safety is also very important in your home with your son. Cover electrical outlets, close up cabinets you don't want your son to have access to and keep your closets clutter free with NO DRY CLEANING PLASTIC!!! Your son could be playing in your closet and fatally harm himself if he gets wrapped up in this dangerous plastic which could smother him. There should be no locked doors in your home; your son could lock himself in one of these rooms. Your son will learn that a closed door requires a knock before opening and entering.

Take advantage of any community workshops that are themed on child safety. Keep emergency phone numbers for poison control, hospital, pediatrician, police and fire departments visible by your phone. Grocery shop in bulk – including all non-food items like toilet tissue and detergent, it is cheaper to buy in bulk rather than going to the corner store everyday, which is marked up in pricing. **Remember** – A clean home is part of the structured environment that your son needs as part of his development. Having a back-up plan is very helpful. Have a very trusted person hold a set of your house keys in case you lock yourself out. Your home is a shared environment with boundaries: this means you have your space and your son has his.

Your home is a sanctuary, a gift from God. Let your son see you clean your home, cook, cry and laugh in your home. Let your home be one of joy and safety that is supported with boundaries. As discussed earlier, any negativity, any actions, persons or things that can jeopardize your home *is not to be tolerated.* Drugs, guns, and certain people are simply not tolerated. To have a drug raid by the police, Child Protective Services do a removal or the police come to your home for domestic violence is a memory that your son will never forget and could have a traumatic impact on him.

The Crying Closet

Home is a sanctuary, to pray and cry in. Keep in mind that your son is not an adult; to process and understand everything relating to adult situations is impossible. An attribute of a black single mother is to LEARN HOW TO CONTROL YOUR EMOTIONS. Check your emotions until you are in a suitable place and time to release. Single parenting requires a strong will; there will be times of disappointment and emotional strain.

I know my son is still a child. I knew the many times the stuff hit the fan and I was emotionally drained – I could NOT open up and emote my emotions in front of my son – he would not understand. Therefore, I had my own "Crying Closet" I used this closet when my son was asleep or out playing with friends. This was my space to let loose to wail and sob. The purging of these emotions in my special space was both healing and very appropriate as I did not want all this negative energy going around my home. Having the one specific place made my feelings all the more bearable. I just gave up my crying closet when my son turned 17. I still have my altar for those high moments of prayer that I use every day.

Spiritual Presence in Your Home.

I am not a religious person but a spiritual one. My parents spent lots of money providing me with a private education that also included theological studies. In my life I have been on my spiritual journey of growth. I am happy to say I have found my niche. My home represents my spirituality. I have an ancestor table with photos and some personal relics of my ancestors. I have African art throughout my home. I also have my spiritual library as well. I am also very fortunate to also have an altar in my home. My black son has seen me pray here and meditate here. My son and I pray together.

I will say this a thousand times – Being a single black mom is challenging! Attending church can be difficult around work schedules and the demands of single parenting (also, many moms are back in school). Participating in church is great and something I enjoy – personally, I do not attend church every Sunday. Physically, I could not attend work, go to school, manage a house, keep up with my son's needs and attend church on a regular basis; with double service.

Emotionally, I have experienced the stigmas of single parenting that have unfortunately extended to the church. SOME churches are very liberal and nurturing single mothers and their children are welcomed with sincerity. Unfortunately, there are other churches that do not. Single mothers are sometimes viewed as man-hunters and home wreckers. The single mother could find herself constantly defending herself in the congregation. For me – the environment hosted unwanted hostility that I just did not want to give my energy to. As I have said before – your baby son is a human sponge and he is soaking up everything around him. We as human beings try not to be judgmental; however in the realm of religion passing judgment does occur. I believe that a person's relationship with God is very personal and intimate – not something to be publicized or scrutinized.

Make your decision about the amount of spiritual exposure you will present to your son. It is important to understand that as part of his development into manhood – it is good for your black son to understand that there is a higher power and to be humble to Him.

Family & Friends Near or Far.

There are many single mothers living without any proximal support (family & friends). Living away from family and support may be by choice or simply fate. Living within close proximity to family and friends is helpful; however the family dynamic must be carefully monitored and boundaries respected. Black single mothers living with extended family has to be mindful that the family order does not change. For example: The black single mother and her son live with the mother's parents. The black son is supported and loved in this sanctuary. The black single mother gets along well with her parents. The black son observes the family order and soon the black son calls the grandmother 'mama.' The family order has absorbed the black single mother and her role as an independent has been absorbed and the *mother unknowingly falls into her old position in the home prior to becoming a mother.*

It is important for the black single mother to maintain her role as primary parent of her son. The black son has to witness the single black mother's authority. It is imperative that the black son maintains his allegiance to his single mother—with the maternal grandparents as support and a vital extension of heritage. The black single mother who lives away from family and friends has the challenge to build support systems to help her be a successful parent. Without the proper support, the black single parent is isolated; this can lead to depression and neglect. Sometimes, family is not what a person in born into, but one that is made through time and trust.

Chapter Four

Relationships

Keepin' it Real.

You are a single black mom of a son – I am going to keep it real and raw in this chapter, so please forgive me in advance, in no way am I intentionally targeting or offending anyone. Life is real, so am I. Motherhood is real...let's GO!

Society instantly perceives you had your son because you are sexually irresponsible. There is no thought to you being a widow, a rape victim, circumstance of failed birth control or a single parent by choice. Society also has quite a few negative expectations of you – the single black mother – unlike the trendy single white moms:

* You, the single black mom are expected to have more children.

* You the single black mom will abuse and neglect your children.

* You, the single black mom are expected to be on welfare with little or no education and no job skill to take care of your black son.

* Your black son is expected to drop out of school and sell drugs.

* Your black son is expected to possess a criminal record at a very young age (9) and be incarcerated before he turns 17 years old.

Historically, the black female was abducted from her homeland where females were revered as queens, leaders, and warriors. Her homeland respected motherhood and its sacredness. In this new world, the black female is seen as an animal to breed and experiment upon with no regard to emotions or outcomes. The black woman has had her babies snatched from her breast and her husband/lover *tasked to sire other children with other women.*

The opportunity of marriage in the traditional sense of monogamy in a nuclear family was taken away. Sex from a master/owner would be the only 'pleasure' known to her. Trauma as the result of this violation has been transferred from generation to generation in the form of stress and illness as well as a breakdown in black relationships. In present day, the black woman is still viewed as a promiscuous sex object with the inability to sustain a viable relationship with a husband or partner.

The black female is regarded as combative, loud and full of attitude. The black female is expected to be nonproductive, sexually irresponsible and a burden on society. The professional black woman today is seen as the oddity; she has to work ten times harder and possess more skills and credentials than a white person or a black male. With all of that hard work, the black male is still preferred and accepted over the black female.

Historically, it has been a challenge for black women to sustain healthy relationships with men because of what was discussed above. Also, it has been drilled into the black woman's head that she needs a man in order to be complete. For example: I have had conversations with other blacks and I am always asked the same two questions: "Who is your husband and what church you belong to?" Single black women are seen as a threat in society because of our strength and versatility. These stigmas make it very challenging to successfully raise a black son in America. No other race/gender is viewed with such disdain as the black female – this goes back as far as the bible.

What Mom Needs: Friendships & the Single Mom

First of all – know yourself – love yourself. You are made in God's image and you are in control of your sexuality. Sex is a gift of responsibility and pleasure. **Sex is NOT the same as love.** Please utilize a safe and reliable method of birth control. As I have stated earlier, please know whom you are having sex with – you could get pregnant, or contract a STI or HIV-AIDS. Friendships are so valuable in life.

It is challenging engaging and maintaining friendships as a single mom. Single mothers are on call 24-7 both physically and financially. Having single or married friends can be challenging as the lifestyles of these two groups are different.

The single black mom is not standoffish nor is she not sociable. The single black mom may not be able to socialize due to financial, support (child care) or time management constraints. The single black mom may be emotionally focused on goals that mean sacrificing a social life at this time—this is okay! It is a wonderful support for single mothers to form groups so their children can play together, even organize their own support group—*it's vital for your black son to see that he is not an oddity being raised by a single parent*—there are others like him. The mothers can support one another in the form of child care pools, mentoring, and many more. The attitude and resiliency of a single mother enriches, motivates, activates and succeeds. There is strength in unity.

Be a Friend to YOURSELF.

Of course accidents occur and not all birth control is 100% reliable unless it is a surgical sterilization. ***Many women I have spoken with feel as though they gave their egg to the wrong man*** and now the woman has to raise their baby alone. I understand the grief of these women; the best remedy for these feelings is to forgive ***oneself and move on.*** Talk with a therapist, mentor, priest/pastor on forgiveness of yourself by yourself. *Never blame your son – he had nothing to do with an act between two adults.* A relationship as black single mom requires trust, responsibility, common sense and tact. There is nothing wrong in getting some sex – just do it the right way:

* USE BIRTH CONTROL!!!

* Go outside of the sanctuary (your home) to have your sexual relations. If you both have to go 50/50 on the hotel room costs – then do it!!! DO NOT BRING MEN HOME FOR SEX WHERE YOU AND YOUR SON LIVE!

* If this sexual partner comes with drama – pass it up! Common sense prevails! YOU HAVE ENOUGH OF YOUR OWN DRAMA – ADDING MORE DRAMA DOES NOT HELP YOU!!!

* Sex does not equate love. Love takes time and patience along with knowledge about the person you have these feelings for. Lust is felt quicker than love.

* Having a man does not complete you! No matter what anyone says!

* Do not engage is risky behaviors (internet sex chats, swinging with couples).

* Trust your gut feelings (instincts) if you do introduce your son to this person.

This person is NOT your son's father. Do not allow this person to discipline your son or make pertinent decisions! – DO NOT GIVE THIS PERSON THAT ROLE. All of this takes time! Frequently in the news are stories of violence against children by the mother's boyfriend. These children are seriously harmed and even killed. As a black mother –

you are responsible for your son's total well being. You are accountable for anything that happens to your son. Don't let alcohol, a wad of cash, good looks or a smooth line link you up to an abuser, controller, dominator.

It is a rare thing to have a man come into the home and raise another man's children like they are from his sperm. The man that does this accepts his woman completely and slowly immerses himself into the family. Remember those nature shows? The new male lion that takes over the pride of female lions kills off every single lion cub that was sired by another lion... It is your responsibility to make sure this man that enters the sanctuary where you and your son live is worthy in every way and can make positive contributions (emotionally, spiritually and financially) to enhance your home and the lives of you and your son.

To raise a black male child to a man requires an enormous amount of **strength**. To be wishy-washy, procrastinate, unorganized or neglectful is going to result in failure. The black woman raising the black male child must be strong in her boundaries, values, and dedication to her son. Motherhood is a thankless position. To the world an articulate, educated, goal focused, black man is an oddity.

Not only do whites remark on your son's abilities but so do fellow blacks – sometimes our own do so in a negative way. It is important that you the black mom shield your son from black on black scrutiny. The scrutiny from fellow blacks is powerful and vicious. How many successful black men have heard that fellow blacks remarked on how they spoke, dressed and behaved was 'selling out,' 'turning white or just 'thinking you are better than us?' Your black son does not have to conform to behaviors that are not positive and uplifting. The amazing thing that will happen is that your son will learn how to live between these two paradigms: your black son will lean to talk and hold mannerisms with the fellas and he will also know how to carry himself in Corporate America.

Another aspect I have encountered as a black single mom is that black single moms are targets for men to repeatedly hit upon and proposition for sexual favors. You are a single black mom – no man is around. No one knows what you do privately because your sexual business is not public. I cannot tell you how many propositions I have had from men for sex (Yes, they have wives and significant others at home!) because I am single and black: one of my son's teachers, the barber at the barbershop, the landlord, men I encountered at my son's karate class and more. Of course I never took any of these men up on their 'offers.' As a result of none of these men knowing the color of my drawers – I was labeled as a *lesbian!* I don't believe I look lonely or desperate. Black single moms – **keep your dignity!**

My son could go anywhere in the community and hold his head up because his mama controlled her sexual power and was discrete with her sexual activity. You can do this as well—what you do in the dark, impacts your black son in the light!

It's great to be in a relationship – no one wants to be alone. The important thing is to recognize and understand timing and control of you. I know it has been said: "The best way to forget one is to get on top of another one." Give yourself time alone to heal and get over a failed relationship. Don't push yourself into the hype of having a man to be complete. There is nothing wrong in being single and focusing on other avenues of your life to build a future for you and your son. Face it – a relationship does possess **distractions** and you must be ready to balance all of that, PLUS your son.

Before you step to a man, please have your emotions sound and get rid of your baggage. Be ready to start anew – leave the past where it belongs – in the past. **Be proud to admit that you are single by choice.** By facing this admission, your life will take on a new meaning of self-elevation, control and focus.

Recently, I watched a talk show where a very popular comedian wrote a book on male/female relationships from the male perspective. The book is very insightful. One woman came onto the show and had a list of requirements/criteria that was very long to the point that the man she is looking for – is not here on this earth. Black single mother I am suggesting that you also look at your own requirements/criteria in searching for a man. Some of your criteria you can satisfy yourself. I am not talking about masturbation - although that is fun and great; I am talking about being your own friend. Some of the criteria women are asking for from a man they can do and should do for themselves. Not as a show of not needing a man, but to exhibit self love. A man may not show his care/love the way you want him to – love yourself and take those criteria, look them over and you will see that you can do and should do some of these things for yourself to yourself.

By reducing the level of expectations, you will take some of the stress off of relationships in your life. Women who have several men at once to fit and address all of her needs; both physical and material – that is another residual behavior from slavery. Basing a person's value on what he can do rather than what he is as a person.

Family and Child Care.

It is important for your son to engage with his family – those who are an *active* part of his life – no matter how small or large. If that is not possible then build a family of trustworthy, positive friends whom share the same goals as you do. Sometimes families are not what you are born into but what you make as you go along in life. Child care is very critical to the single black mom. Choose a reliable system and **please pick your son up on time!** It is a terrible feeling to be the last kid left and believe me – when you are late – negative things are assumed and your son does get a sense of abandonment. If you leave your son anywhere, day care or school and you do not come to pick him up by a certain time of closing – that provider has the right to take your son to the local police department and you may face an investigation by Child Protective Services for neglect/abandonment. PAY YOUR CHILD CARE PROVIDER!!! Child care is an extension of mom care and is just as valuable. We have already discussed the family dynamics that can occur if you were to move back home in a previous chapter.

Affection and the Black Son.

Building your son's self esteem is vital to his manhood. Offer him praise; do not call him negative names. Listen to him. The black mom with the black son must possess strength to be prepared for whatever may come in regard to her son: that phone call, letter or ringing door bell places the black mother on point and you better be ready! If someone compliments you on your son's attributes – thank them – it is a historical habit that black parents minimize and down play compliments given to their children. This originates from slavery where the child who was praised was taken from his mother and sold.

There is nothing wrong in being proud and praising your son!

You and your son live in your sanctuary that is clean, organized and easily managed. The professional or welfare mom can have what I have discussed so far – it takes *work*. The important thing is your son's appropriate *role* he has in his sanctuary – his home. Your son is NOT the man of the house! Your son is a child who does not possess the maturity and common sense of an adult. DO NOT give your son the role of 'little man' – let him be a child for as long as he can!

Consequently, your son is NOT a fashion accessory! Dressing him so he looks like Diddy or 50 Cent is inappropriate. Your black son is a child, not a fad or a celebrity – save that stuff for Halloween if you want. Dress your son for safety, comfort and practicality. Save that extra money spent of designer labels and put that money towards your son's education.

Your son is NOT the absentee father/boyfriend/husband. Even if your son strongly resembles his father – he is your son and a child.

Maintain the proper boundaries in your son's identity and place in the family. Your son will grow to embrace his place in life – as a king without negative associations that will break down his self esteem.

The relationship between you and your son is so very important because how your relationship is with your son will determine how well your son relates to the world. It is necessary to be strong, command respect, maintain boundaries and be organized. At the same time, you **MUST** practice what you preach – your son needs to see you **LIVING** what you are saying. If you don't want your son to lie – then don't lie to him. If you want your son to be articulate then speak clearly to him with no slang, Ebonics or baby talk.

Remember – children live by example. Let your son see you pray, laugh and cry (different than the crying closet). When the sofa dropped on my foot – my son saw me cry!

Do not let your son witness you smoking, having sex or getting your ass kicked! If you have to open a can of ass whipping on someone – try NOT to do this in front of your son. It is important for your son to trust you and therefore you must be trustworthy.

You must exhibit manners: 'Please', 'Thank you' and 'I am sorry' go a long way. If you can volunteer in your community. Let your son see you studying, in fact study together. Allow your son to share in your education experience. Expose your son to your hobbies or discover new ones with him.

I kissed and hugged my son for hours when he was a baby. I chewed up his food for him (hot dogs) before he ate it. I smiled and sang to him every chance I got. What I am trying to say is just because your child is a boy – you should NOT be emotional detached or be 'hard' with your son so he will 'man up.' Your son needs emotion, your presence and affection – your son will take great comfort in having these things from you. There is nothing sexual about giving your son love and affection. An affectionate black man had exposure to love and affection in his upbringing. This stays with him for life.

Our black children are chameleons; they adapt to any circumstance and environment. Your son will learn as he matures when to be hard and when to be sensitive. There is a healthy balance between the two. Your son does not have to be a thug to be a man. Your son needs to be a human being: Caring, sensitive, aware and accountable. Be respectful of others and of himself. By providing that affection on a continual basis to your black son will shape his life to one of giving, forgiving and positive living!

Protection and the Black Son.

Safety and protection are fundamentals for a young black child. Your son needs to feel safe and protected. As an infant, you protected your son and kept him safe – these actions need to continue well into manhood. Safety is a discussion about sex, drugs, gangs, violence, guns, peer pressure and so much more. Protection is self defense with logical thought, common sense and boundaries. Enrolling your son into a karate class at a young age is very helpful for self-esteem building, burning off energy, physical exercise and your son will be able to defend himself if he has to fight. What if a girl hits your son? Do you want your son hitting girls? These discussions are vital. Your son will encounter these scenarios by being in school, camp and day care.

Your black son needs to feel protected, as he grows up – he will protect whom he cares about. Your home should be the safe sanctuary that you have made it – We have already discussed this topic in prior chapters. There is another avenue of protection – Having Your Black Son's Back that will be fully discussed in a future chapter.

Safety and being the protector was taken from the black man from slavery when he could not protect his family, his children; his black queen. Think about it; women are attracted to men whom offer protection: sexually, financially, emotionally & physically. It is vital that your black son grows up practicing protecting black females: using condoms during sex, avoiding physical violence, verbal, emotional violence against women and not allowing the black woman to be in any dangerous/vulnerable circumstances. Your black son's first experience with this is YOU.

The black male has to embrace the role of protector. Leaders Protect, your son must learn how to protect as well. Your black son learns how to protect from you protecting him. Feeling safe in one's own skin: The media does not portray black men in a positive light. Black males are almost always depicted as violent gang members, drug dealers, prisoners, pimps, or mentally unstable. Your black son absorbs what he hears from you; about his father and black men as a whole. You that black single mom must be aware of what is being said around your son. Having inappropriate conversations around your son is NOT allowed. At the same time, your black son needs to see black males in roles of power and success; have your black son acknowledge these men. Negative communication, male bashing and derogatory actions against the absentee father does nothing positive for your son. You placing the absentee father through all kinds of drama: cursing him out in front of your son, tricking him in family court for financial gain – all of these actions you are doing you black son is witnessing and the result is staggering .

As a result, your black son grows up with a personal vow: To never be treated like how his father is being treated by a black woman (you). You son festers hatred and anger towards this black woman because of the anger and hatred he is witnessing from you (violence begets violence) – as a result, your black son develops negative feelings or mistrust, hatred and anger towards black women. Your black son will grow up abusing black women, harbor resentment and possess a tangible resentment towards black women – all because of what he has witnessed from you. Is there any wonder why some black men continue to act negatively towards black women today? Today I see quite a few of black men ignore black women, abandon black women, demean and abuse black women. Where did this behavior originate from? Slavery.

Communication.

In sound, healthy relationships there is communication. You are so close to your son that you can understand his baby talk. Keep talking with your son as he grows up – ask him what went on in his day – listen to what he has to say. I have always raised my son in talking - just having a conversation that is engaging and at the same time informative for me as a parent. My son and I talk about *anything;* sex, girls, drugs, friends, school, clothes, what he saw on the walk home from school – anything. I would rather have my son come and ask me questions as opposed to getting the *wrong* information out on the streets. If my son asks me something and if I don't know the answer – I will research it and find the answer for him.

Being active in my son's life is a form of parenting that is democratic; my son has *some* input and reactions and I am an active participant. My son's input and reactions grow as he matures and shows responsibility with common sense.

Black moms should also participate in their black son's activities. Yes, the class guinea pig stayed in our house over Christmas break. Yes, I sat through the Power Rangers Show at Radio City Music Hall. Yes, I know every Barney song and Author episode. Yes, I know most of the first Pokemon characters – I still find myself humming some of the Disney movie songs and on rare occasions when I do turn on my television – I love watching cartoons. I have hosted boy's nite sleepovers and I was a permanent fixture at my son's school through 12th grade.

Being a participating parent brings the extra bond; that awareness of whom is interacting with your son and how. By being a participating parent also gave my son a sense of security. Have you ever seen the face of a child whose parent does not show up on parent conference/visit day? I made the **sacrifice** of using vacation time, working through lunch and even taking a few hours pay cut in order to do these things – but it was worth it.

Teachers respect and respond to the kid whose parent participates (I will talk more about this in the

Education Chapter). There is no other love like a mother's love, no other care that is more healing than the care of a parent who is committed. Your active participation PROFESSES your love, and importance in your black son's life. You are taking ownership and believe me, your son is so very proud = what a self– esteem builder!

I Pledge Allegiance to My Mom!!!

You and your son are close – you have worked hard on building trust and communication. Allegiance is also very important; it is defined as **devotion** or **loyalty** to a person, group, or cause. Your son has to be loyal to you and you to him. Your son has to be comfortable in coming to you to guide him and make decisions. When your son is presented with an invitation, gift or idea – he should come to his mom for your okay. Here are a few examples:

Your son gets an invite to go to a birthday party – instead of immediately accepting – he comes to you with the invite and asks if he can go. A friend or relative wants to buy your son a pair of skates – your son does not immediately accepts but calls you to see if it is okay to accept the gift. Your son is part of a youth group that requires the teens to buddy up with each other and attend practice. The facilitator directs your son and his buddy to coordinate on how to get to practice. Your son says that you, his mom has to be a part of the coordination process so that he and his buddy can get to practice.

The allegiance between you and your son is respect. It is trust and it is love. That bond grows as you both get older and that bond is impenetrable. My son knows I am loyal to him and he is to me. People who know my son and I (family, friends & community) also know this. This power and control is very positive and supportive as a parent in every way. Nothing goes to your son unless you are aware of it and/or it goes through you.

I often think of this model as a biblical example of John 14:6 "Jesus said to him, I am the way, the truth and the life. No one comes to the Father except through me."

Not to sound blasphemous or disrespectful in any way – but this bible verse speaks exactly to my beliefs in the allegiance between the single black mom and her black son. You as a black mom are not to be so quick to hand off your responsibility of being a mom of your black son to another person such as a boyfriend or other family member – **do not let the system take your black son and raise him** – this responsibility was given to **you**! In turn, if anyone is communicating any kind of short cut that diminishes your position/role as parent, do not allow it. Call this person out on their behavior and politely remind them that you are the parent and you will make the decisions. You the parent have authority and a responsibility that holds you accountable for your black son's life in ALL aspects. You must be fully aware of what is being done to your son and by whom and where as much as possible!

Strengthening Your Son With Words.

You have a black child, a son. I don't care if he is adopted, surrogated, foster or biological – there are some very important words you NEED to tell your son at LEAST once a day:

* **I love you** – This is so important: Your son must feel that he is loved and he is wanted by you. I don't care if he came as a surprise – your son has to hear that he is wanted and loved by **you**!

* **You Are So Very Important To Me and This World**: A black son will grow up to become a black man. This sentence provides positive support. Believe it or not,

this affirmation you give to your son will repeat itself in his mind. When your son is faced with doing something inappropriate/wrong – this affirmation will come into his mind and reduce the chance of him going through with that destructive act that will harm him and his future. YOU value your black son; Your black son values himself, he will be more watchful of what he is doing, saying and where he is.

    * **I Am Sorry**: Be accountable, show your black son accountability and watch him take accountability on his own. It is very difficult for some people to say 'I am sorry' – but these words are very powerful. Always identify what you are sorry about.

It is vital to say these three statements to build your son's self esteem and inner worth. If your son knows someone truly cares and values him – he will value himself and NOT look for validation in the wrong places (gangs).

    Communication as I have described will strengthen your son's spirit, dreams, and respect for others. Communication with your son will always include those 'boy questions': finding out the whys about things you never thought of. Communication in the ways I have discussed will help your son with the genetically inherited effects of slavery. By verbalizing to your black son his worth and value will result in him doing actions that are worthwhile and valuable.

With a strong foundation of communication between you and your son gives you (the parent) the advantage of knowing your son to the point that if anyone approaches you and tells you something about your son – you won't have any doubts because of the bond of trust between your son and you is strong. If your son does do something – he will come to you first – before anyone else does and tell you what he has done himself. I prefer this as opposed to hearing about anything my son has done from someone else. I have communicated this preference to my son – he knows it is best if he tells me first as opposed to me hearing it from someone else. Sure, it may be wrong and it may make me angry, but it is best for the communication to come from my son than from the street. This teaches the black son to own up to his actions and is a skill he will take into adulthood.

Your black son will be able to speak for himself when you are not present – he will be able to advocate and use common sense. His confidence in the belief that he is loved and valued will deter him from making dangerous and destructive choices – Let's face it; the number one reason why a black male joins a gang is to get that love, validation and protection. Why not save your son's life and give him these things at home from **you**!

The opposite occurs with the black son who is not strengthened with words. Inability to express himself results in lashing out, anger, violent behaviors, low self esteem, making poor choices on friendships and actions; inability to sustain good, healthy relationships because of poor communication, unable to embrace success, self disfigurement, spiritually un-centered, inability to respect authority or set goals. This can result in depression and even a criminal record. Arm and fortify your black son with words and praise of encouragement. These few, simple sincere words will elevate your black son to become the king he is meant to become. I can also guarantee you; your strengthening words will be returned to you by your black son. He will praise you as you praise him; together you both praise GOD!

When the Shit Hits the Fan!

Picture the old Airplane! Movie – when you see a large fan on the screen and someone throws a large amount of horse manure at it – splat! Shit flies all over the place!

Oh this will happen a lot! Boys will be boys and mom will right there to straighten them out! My son is the only person who can make me laugh the hardest, cry the longest and make my head pop off in anger (I am a Leo!). As a rule I do practice the following:

* I NEVER physically discipline my son in public! I have seen black mothers come into their child's school and whip their son's asses! I find this to be demeaning. I have also observed that some adults purposefully incite the parents so they can watch the child get hit as a thrill for the adult. The beaten black son also now has to face his peers the next day after he got beat in front of everyone by his mom. *Haven't blacks been beaten, hung and torched enough in public?* Black mom – keep yourself calm – find out all the facts and wait until you get home to discipline your son!

* NEVER discipline your son with food. Never withhold a meal from your son as a form of punishment. Never use food as a form of comfort either.

* Make it a point to exhibit self-control in tense situations so that your black son models your actions in attempting to keep a level head when stress arises.

* Allow your black son to advocate for himself first; then you step in.

* I teach my son that being a 'thug' or 'gangsta' belongs only in one place – a music video for entertainment purposes only...

Parenting is not about you the mom – it is about your son and his needs and how his needs are responded to by you. It is the mother's responsibility as the single black female to respondto her black son's needs and think of her needs later – in other words – she deals with the issue concerning her son and then personally reacts (puke, cry) later.

Let's talk some more about discipline. A black mother who has an 11 year old son gave me some insight on discipline after her own experience. Today's children are surrounded by talk of child abuse and Child Protective

Services. School staff and child care providers are all mandated reporters. Time and time again I have heard of children threatening their parent/guardian with reporting them to CPS when they are disciplined. The result, parents are wary of disciplining their children for fear of being reported or investigated. As this mother explained to me:

"I was never spoken to by my son's teacher or principal: my son did have a behavior issue that was related to a change in my household. My son also had bronchitis that kept him up at night and he was not rested enough for school the following day. All of these things may have appeared suspicious and the teacher and principal questioned my son by asking opened ended questions. Child Protective Services was called on my family not once but *twice*. It was only when I called a meeting at the school after these two investigations took place on me and my entire family that I was able to find out the origin of how these investigations came to be. The teacher never notified me or my husband of any behavior changes in my son in the classroom and my son's behavior was **assumed** to be related to some abuse at home. CPS questioned each member of my family, even my daughter who is away at college and was not physically present in the home at the time. My husband could have lost his state job and I would have lost my two foster children all because of a lack of communication and now the school's administration is aware that I have spanked my son in the past. Now, if he comes to school looking 'slightly suspicious' it is assumed that my son was abused at home. My son knew nothing of CPS and abuse until this happened. Now he talks about abuse all the time and he questions both his mom and dad. I feel as though every action as a parent that I do is under scrutiny – I cannot discipline my son now because of this entire thing. My son talks about CPS all the time."

I have also heard of children actually calling the police when the parents discipline them. Yes, Child Protective Services is a very good entity, but where is the boundary between parents trying to be accountable and parents who are being abusive? Such a phenomenon has diminished parent's ability to discipline their children in order to avoid such occurrences. The result – children are left to run amok and there isn't any behavior moderation; society and schools complain that these children have no self control and no respect of authority. Yes, there are abused children out there and they need protection. However, when a parent has to question his/her authority over their own child and even avoid discipline because of the above. Parents must have some authority.

This is a vicious cycle; the child is expected to behave and yet parents cannot discipline. When the child behaves badly, the parent is blamed. The most popular recourse I have seen is the child being taken to the pediatrician and given Ritalin because "Larry is not behaving like the other kids." Larry does not need Ritalin;

he needs boundaries and a learned sense to respect authority. **Ritalin is a life-long label.** I will say it again: Ritalin is a life -long label. Giving your son Ritalin places him in a category that excludes him from future opportunities: The government will want to know your sons medical history from childhood for a job, **Ritalin use is a red flag.** The Armed Services notices this as well. Be very careful of asking for any behavior modification medications for your son without the proper testing to verify the need before getting that prescription.

I was raised before the era of CPS: Blacks can describe whippings and beatings from their childhood like no one else can. Many attribute this to slavery – black slaves were beaten and disfigured all in the name of discipline. I am dead set against any kind of corporal punishment that involves punching, beating with extension cords, etc. I do believe children do need to be spanked on their bottoms. There may be a time where you may have to handle your son forcefully if he is having a tantrum or so angry that he is not listening and he is danger of hurting himself or others.

I do not believe in giving up punishment totally. Have your son sit and write out his punishment, take away the TV, games and play time. It is important that your son understands the cause and effect principle: Your son does something bad, he is punished *and* forgiven. The systems around your son are all mandated reporters and are doing their job. In the instances where the abuse is found and a child's life is saved makes all the inconveniences worth it.

As for the example with the acquaintance, there was a way she may have been able to possibly avoid the above: Once your black son is home with you for the evening, the teacher and the school has no way of knowing what is going on at home unless you the parent notify them. A simple note to the teacher about the son's change in family household as well as his illness may have helped the situation. More will be discussed in the Education Chapter.

(In any communication you send to your son's school – always put a contact phone number where you can be reached and the date).

Violence and your black son are NOT synamous. If you are violent with your black son, he will emote the same behavior that was done to him. Violence is an act that is not positive. In school, violence and tantrums are noted and your black son gives up control due to his behavior. Your black son is now monitored, expelled from school or undergo a psychological evaluation. He may even have police charges pressed against him. These behaviors are noted in his file and your black son's validity decreases.

Violence is simply not tolerated. In prison violence is dealt with by placing the inmate in solitary confinement. In the world, the community slowly isolates your violent son until he is in prison in solitary confinement. Your black son emulating gangsters, drug dealers or prisoners without fully understanding the origin or potential social/personal consequences is dangerous. Judge Greg Mathis says: *"Copying prisoners can contribute to a prisoner mentality. Already our young men refer to a prison stint as a state-paid 'vacation' or time away at 'school.' Prison is not luxurious and the education received there will not serve the inmate well once he returns home. Prison has become, for many, an unfortunate rite of passage."**

*Mathis, Greg. "The Sad Truth About Saggin' Pants." Ebony Magazine July 2008 Pg. 42.

Discipline and boundaries are very important for the black son. Society judges blacks more harshly than other races, so many of our black men are implicated for crimes they did not do – only to waste 10, 15, 20, 25 years or more in prison and be found innocent based on DNA. It's time to stop making the prison stock shareholder rich off of our black men. Kings do not belong in prison.

Money – The Prince's Lot to Being a King.

I am a black single mom – I am the clearance, coupon using, layaway, sale seeking, return merchandise, reward points grabbing, early door buster, buy one get two free rebate queen! I look for ways to save money and make my dollar go further! You can do it too. I *love* getting a deal! Over the years I have made shopping into a game of how much I can save.

Traditionally, few blacks inherent any material wealth, but tons of emotional stress! Money is a major factor in your black son's life and therefore YOU are the one who will introduce him to the concepts and facts about money. It is helpful to pay yourself through your 401K and your salary; you can even enroll in a Holiday Club at your local bank. If you don't have one, open up a savings account and buy certificates of deposit, stocks or invest in real estate. Always have a little side hustle going on with yourself. Let your black son see you being productive and comfortable with finances – I don't mean just lamenting about your bills. *Put aside money for your son's education.*

I know – money is TIGHT! I have lived paycheck to paycheck since I became a single parent. My credit score is a mess; my score matches my weight and yes I too have made terrible financial decisions in the past because of lack of knowledge. Become savvy in finances. DO NOT USE CREDIT CARDS!!!! Let your checking account be linked to a debit card. If you don't have the money in your account that is linked to that card – you cannot spend!

If there are classes offered in financial planning in your community - TAKE THEM. There are a few hard working black women who are single moms and have made it a personal mission to elevate and educate other black single moms in the world of finance: Samantha Gregory has a website: Richsinglemomma.com and Dr. Elon Bomani www.thedynamicdiva.com check out these two powerful websites and be ready to learn! Of course – Oprah has Suze Orman.

I have witnessed black mothers not give their black sons a little pocket money because they don't want their son's to buy junk. Here are my views on black son's and money:

* Give your son an allowance and guide him on how to spend it – action and consequences. If you don't give your son a little pocket money – the drug dealers will. The earlier your son is used to handling money, the more comfortable he will be with money and the less influence money will have over him.

* Teach your son to save. This helps your son to project this mind towards a future. In my home we have an 'Emergency Spot' a place where a small amount of money is kept for emergencies. If I dip into it – I have to replace whatever I took out – the same thing goes for my son.

* Your black son must understand the dynamics of money = power. New money cuts your fingers, when money is old it stinks. When you do not have money – you miss it like hell. Fools and money is not a good match. In today's world – money does not talk – it screams. Money is to be respected. *Nothing comes for free.*

*Your black son's relationship with money from an early age will stay with him through adulthood. A man who understands money has control, respect and common sense. Money does not respect fools or greed – do not let your son be controlled by money.

* Hey! That is your son's Social Security number - NOT YOURS!!! Please do not use your son's social security number to get a phone line, cable television or a credit card. I have seen mothers do this – what you are doing is wrecking your son's credit before he is age two! Your son grows to be a good man and goes out into the world with a credit report that looks like hell – thanks to you! If your credit line is shot to hell then bring it back up with time, patience and sacrifice. Simply do without - but do not put your son's future at risk by using his social security number and his credit.

She Works Hard For the Money!

I talked earlier about how black women are viewed in society earlier, so I am going keep movin'! Thank goodness for the companies who support single parenting! Today's employer wants employees to be successful but many employers do not support philanthropic endeavors or parenting. Imagine if employers supported mentoring and volunteering in communities! Single mothers have a challenge – a black single mother has a greater challenge. Not only is the black single mom paid less than whites, she has to work harder.

The corporate world embraces the black male quicker than the black female. The black female has witnessed all through her life white women in positions of power that they are not qualified for, not educated enough for and are not suited for. A prime example of this is the 2008 Republican Vice President candidate Sarah Palin. How is it possible that a woman with a Bachelor's Degree in Journalism is Governor of a state and then selected to be a Republican Vice President Candidate for a country? How is it possible that a person with absolutely no background in law is chosen to build, uphold and protect laws of an entire country? Do you think Mrs. Palin worries about childcare? Does Mrs. Palin worry about affording housing or paying her bills? I don't think so! Michelle Obama has a Doctorate Degree in Law and has been viewed very harshly! THINK ABOUT THIS!!!

The black single mother has to maintain a certain mindset in order to be a successful single working parent:

* Vacation and sick days are NOT yours – this time is kept for your son in case he is sick or you are needed at his school.

* Your son's needs are going to fall upon your shoulders. Get used to this and organize yourself so that you and your son are successful and the accomplishments appear effortless.

* Have a good, reliable emergency contact person in case you can't get away from work.

*Get your son's school calendar at the beginning of the school year and schedule needed time off in advance for your son's education support.

* Keep urgent contact phone numbers handy at your job so that you have your son's school, childcare, pediatrician and emergency

contact person's phone numbers all in one spot – ready for you when you need them.

* Communicate to your employer that your family's health and well being is a priority to you.

*There will be plenty of skipped lunches and make up times that you will have to give your employer but your son is worth it!

* Do not use your single parenthood status as an excuse or crutch to get time off from work. Do not abuse the assistance you are given. * Take your tax refund and use it to pay for camp and childcare during the summer.

I did not take a vacation until my son was eight years old and that was when my mom sent us to Disney World. I have always kept my vacation and sick time for my son's needs – a day off for me was one of the few given paid national holidays recognized by my employer. Usually, my son had these days off from school as well!

If you can also secure a person who can watch your son while he is ill at home is great. A mild illness is ok to have him at home with a safe child-care provider. Many parents send their children off to school and childcare with green noses, vomiting, red eyes, fevers and wet coughs. Please keep your son at home and let him rest and recuperate in his familiar surroundings. It is cruel to your child and to the other children he is around to send him to school or childcare when he is sick and contagious.

My employer at every job I have ever held was made aware that my son is my priority and if he is ill or in distress in any way – I will be there for him. I have lost a few jobs over this but I have my son safe and healthy not abandoned and neglected. I have thought about the great jobs I could have had that paid much more but would have demanded that I be away from my son and not be accessible if he needed me – this was simply not an option for me. I tried it: working at a high paying job that required a commute away from home and community as well as long hours – that was a very dark time of motherhood for me and I promised my son and myself that I would never do that again. My son is off to college now; I can do more with my career. As a black single mom I am near my son, accessible and participating in every aspect of his life as I should be. Please make time to really think about your career, the demands and being a black single mother to your son.

Remember – no one will take care of your son and know all of his traits like you do. There is nothing like a mother's love and presence.

Teaching your black son to be a latch key kid today is very different that when I was growing up. Back in the day – the neighborhood I grew up in was made up of familiar faces where everyone knew everyone. The elders looked out for the young and if your parents even hear that you did something wrong – you were in BIG trouble!

The neighborhoods today are made up of a transient population as many people move more frequently due to high costs of rent/mortgages. It is more challenging today to get to know your neighbors. Your black son will be a latch key child – he has to abide by certain rules to help him and you:

* Communication – If your son stays after school or goes somewhere with a friend he needs to tell you.

* Give your son a cell phone for emergencies only – stores now carry cell phones

just for kids and are programmed for certain numbers only.

* Don't let your son carry his house keys dangling from his neck. The keys are visible and a beacon for predators. Have him wear his keys under his shirt or hooked onto his pants.

* Your son must call you once he is in the house on the house phone – use caller ID so you can verify that he called you from home.

* Your son must understand that he is NOT TO OPEN THE DOOR FOR ANYONE FOR ANY REASON ONCE IS INSIDE THE HOUSE.

* Your son is NOT to go near the door to answer if anyone rings the bell or knocks.

* Establish a safety regiment with your son for after school until you get home.

* Have a snack ready for him. Instruct him that he is NOT to use the stove, plug in anything or use matches for any reason.

*Be mindful about what age you think your son can be a latch key child. A young child at home without an adult can be viewed as a form of neglect.

* Think of the investments of child care – soon your son will be old enough and responsible to be home for a few hours until you get off from work.

* Company – other kids in your home with your son while you are out of the house is simply not acceptable. No friends can come over until adult supervision is in your home.

* Your special needs child should not be left alone—please have proper supervision in place at all times.

Your black son is your responsibility – the time, effort and level of expense you invest will be the level of satisfaction, ease and comfort you will have. These actions require sacrifice, and your presence – YOU cannot be substituted by anyone else! Child care is not forever (in most cases) and with registered child care providers – you can claim this expense on your taxes – consult with your accountant!

I'm Ok with me – You Be Ok with me too!

There have been countless times throughout being a single mother that I have had friends & acquaintances whom have tried to fix me up with a friend or relative as a potential boyfriend. These people took it upon themselves to attempt to change my social status. I never asked any of these people to introduce me to anyone. In my daily outside life, I keep my social life personal; a few quick jokes occasionally but my private life is private. My personal appearance also never indicated that I wanted such actions.

I am a single black mom but I have also made sure that I included a regime of self-care in my lifestyle: I watch my weight continuously, I keep my hair, skin and nails groomed, I visit the dentist twice a year, I read up on current issues and I love museums and such. I guess to some I am a catch – I take good care of my son and myself, so I must be able to take care of a man!

Friends and acquaintances that have introduced me to their brothers, cousins and friends have to understand that I am happy with me and they should be happy with me too. All of the men I was introduced to were nice in their own right, but not husband, boyfriend or significant other material. Yes, I am a supreme caretaker, but single moms are not destined to be caretakers for life! We want to be cared for as well.

Black single mom, don't feel obligated to go along with your family, friends and acquaintances that are persistent in trying to fix you up with someone because "You need a man." Maintain your stance on your comfort with your social status. The many times I was fixed up, I was not ready for a relationship. I was focused on my son and evolving myself to the woman that I am today. I am in love with myself more now that I was ten years ago, I am also not the same woman I was ten years ago.

Black single moms – don't rush up on a relationship – give yourself time and give your black son all of your focus as you possibly can. There is nothing wrong with having a relationship – but it is time consuming and distracting. I don't think I could have accomplished all that I have if I were in a relationship. I have found fulfillment in my work and being a single mom. Remain firm with family, friends and acquaintances on your comfort with your own social status. Be very selective on whom you choose to be your man. In order to be loved – you must love yourself first. Heal, grow, learn and relax before rushing into a relationship – don't EVER believe that a man completes you or that you need a man in your home.

Read up on relationships, Steve Harvey's book "Act like a Lady, Think like a Man" is an excellent and sincere look at relationships. Personally, I have faith in God that my soul mate and I will find one another. Now that my son is off to college he is encouraging me to date and I do have the flexibility and maybe a **little** time to do just that! Have faith and stay focused on your black son. Love yourself and love will come to you.

Chapter Five

Education

Education Saves Lives.

Education saves lives, strengthens character and broadens a person's vision of life. There is an old negative saying: "If you want to keep a secret from a black man, put it in a book because blacks' don't read." While Africans were taken away from their homeland and forced into slavery, slaves were forbidden to learn how to read and write. This outlaw certifies just how powerful education is. The slave in the Unites States of America, our ancestors fought to be educated which was denied to them, evolving into the educated Negro, the learned black, the African American Scholar and finally the first Black President of the United States Barak Obama.

Our ancestors saw education as an opportunity to break the chains of stigma, segregation and status that were ascribed to blacks from slavery. Blacks advocated for integrated education, formed black collages, fraternities and sororities to support one another in higher education. There was a time when education was a distinction of honor held by a black man; there was a time when a book was valued and not destroyed/ignored.

There was a time when a school was a place to learn and teachers taught. Today's generation has reacted to the change in education resulting from the advancement of technology. Students today rely on a computer, not the Dewey Decimal System for obtaining information; children rip up and write in books, teachers are caseworkers and 'academic entertainers'; protected by contracts and unions. The school system is now modeled and functioning similar to 'junior prisons' where test scores determines a child's future, not family tradition or personal dreams. Schools are no longer a sanctuary, but a place where violence and discrimination have become a business.

Our ancestors fought and died for this? Why do some blacks embrace education only *after* they are assigned an orange suit and an identification number? Education is an inherent right of every person in this country white or black. Historically, Nobel Peace Prize Recipient Dr. William Shockley tried to scientifically justify that blacks were inferior as far as learning aptitude and intellect versus whites. The Moynihan Papers* would describe the breakdown of families; consideration must be given to the fact that black children grow up in more economic distressed environments that contribute to poor educational outcomes.

The Negro Family: The Case For National Action, also known as the **Moynihan Report**, named after U.S. Senator Daniel Patrick Moynihan, the author of the controversial report, was released in 1965. It hypothesized that the destruction of the Black nuclear-family structure would hinder further progress towards economic, and political equality.

The Moynihan Report: Why are Black Families in Crisis?

Daniel Patrick Moynihan argues in his 1965 report that the roots of black families' problems lie in the legacy of slavery, growing ubanization, discrimination, and a tradition of matriarchy. Unlike whites, 1960's black families in the U.S., particularly in urban areas, are approaching "total breakdown," writes Daniel Patrick Moynihan in his 1965 report *The Negro Family: The Case for National Action*. Despite an emerging black middle class, conditions for lower-income black families continue to worsen and are likely to continue to do so, warns the author. He says that the roots of black families' problems lie in: the legacy of slavery, growing urbanization, traditional black family structure, and discrimination in employment and education.

Dehumanization Through Slavery

Slavery in the U.S. has had a greater long-term impact than slavery in other countries such as Brazil because of the American traditions of English law and Protestant religion. Since neither could justify human bondage, Moynihan says that white Americans reduced black slaves to non-humans or "chattels." Slave in Brazil and other feudal countries were still seen as human beings. American slaves had no claim to their children, spouses, or native religion. Emancipation of the slaves gave blacks liberty but not equality. Moynihan says that emancipation began an era of "keeping the Negro in his place." This overt white domination had a more destructive impact on black males than females, he adds, as it stymied the emergence of strong black leadership figures.

Rapid Urbanization Leads to Slums

The rapid movement of American people from rural to urban areas caused disruption to "traditional social patterns," says

Moynihan. He notes the emergence of Irish slums in the 1800s and then black slums a century later. However, key differences exist: Black families are more often headed by a single mother in urban than in rural areas. Middle-class blacks cannot escape the slums because of housing discrimination. In northeastern urban areas, 26% of once-married black women are divorced, separated or have absent husbands. Urban illegitimacy rates are higher than non-urban rates.

Matriarchy Sets Black Families Apart Not only are black families more likely to be headed by a woman than whites, but even in married couples the wife is a stronger presence. Moynihan cites a study by Robert Blood and Donald Wolfe, who found that 44% of wives in black families in Detroit were "dominant" compared to 20% of wives in white families. This matriarchal structure, says Moynihan, is passed on to children and results in greater achievements among black women. For example: Black women tend to be better educated than black men. Black women are better represented in white collar and professional jobs than black men.

Family Breakdown Leads to Social Meltdown In his report, Moynihan argues that declining unemployment also has contributed to black family breakdown. Family breakdown, in turn, has contributed to rising rates of illegitimacy, welfare dependency, school dropout, and crime. The result is one of the most serious and potentially explosive problems facing America. Moynihan concludes that a concerted national effort is needed to strengthen the black family to help blacks take advantage of emerging opportunities.

Research Design:

"The Roots of the Problem" and "The Tangle of Pathology" are the third and forth chapters respectively of *The Negro American Family: The Case for National Action,* written by Daniel Patrick Moynihan. The book includes data from the Bureau of Labor.

Statistics and from several U.S. Censuses. At the time it was written, the author was the assistant secretary at the U.S. Department of Labor.

Citation: This Keytext reports some of the ideas and findings from the following source: Moynihan, D. P. (1965). *The negro family: The case for national action.* U.S. Department of Labor. Retrieved October 17, 2002 from http://www.dol.gov/asp/programs/history/webid-meynihan.htm

Interestingly enough, the educational plight of

blacks is related to slavery, family break down and women

as head of black households. I felt it vital to include the

above in the hopes of inciting readers to support black

young men. To embrace education is to embrace one's

spirit: to demonstrate humility, dedication and sacrifice.

Blacks must renounce instant gratification and unify as our

ancestors did.

The No Child Left Behind Model of education in

America has resulted in the highest growth of the need for

more prisons and special education programs more than

ever. Someone has profited greatly on No Child Left

Behind and it's not the blacks. It is time for blacks to place

value back in education where it belongs. The lack of

success in education today for our youth is a form of

slavery that has evolved from what our ancestors endured.

Absence of strong practices in education has targeted our

youth to be unsuccessful, unproductive and non-

contributory to themselves and society.

Until the United States of America places a

consistent, proactive value on education from Head Start

to college graduation, our black youth will continue to struggle and do poorly. Prisons are being built faster than schools.

Black women have always understood the value and history of education. This understanding must be passed onto our black sons. Accessibility to education is present: grants, scholarships and loans are available. Keep our black sons out of prison and in school. "It takes a village to raise a child." This African Proverb existed long before Senator Hilary Clinton made it a political campaign slogan.

Education demands dedication, and self discipline in the home that is exhibited in the schools where teachers teach and administrators understand the duty of educating children today is the best sound investment for a future any race can be proud of. The black male child is expected to fail the school system – I have mentioned this earlier, from an early age – the black male child must be exposed to education and be shown the appreciation in the value of education. From the beginning – do not let your son destroy his storybooks by writing in them or tearing them up! To this day my son and I donate any books we have at home and we also donate to the local library, jail or school library. Books are to be valued for the knowledge they hold. How many black homes have bookshelves with books on them? Learning about black history is also very important in raising the black child. Black history is not just in the USA but the world.

Education is the job of both parent and child. Your son needs an early start to his education – this start begins with you and ends with you when he goes off to college and you sign for his financial aid! Get your son counting, reading, organizing, recognize his shapes and colors. Teach your son how to write his name before he enters Pre Kindergarten. Children now have to take a test before entering Pre-K to determine aptitude – you don't want your son left behind. *It is important for you as the black single mom to put your own negative experiences with education aside (if you have any) and start anew with your son.*

Remember – children learn by example. I recently viewed a HBO special: "The Black List." Vernon Jordan was discussing his childhood. His mother became president of the school PTA. Mr. Jordan stated that his mother Mrs. Jordan believed that: "Through her presence and participation, this would make things better for **all** boys, not just her sons." I could not agree more with this statement. Whenever I participated in any way at my son's school, my son was proud of my presence but at the same time my presence uplifted other black young boys. These princes looked forward to my hugs, my words of encouragement and my advocacy. Imagine if 20 more black mothers became involved and were present at the schools, how well would our son's be? Reading at a young age takes determination and stimulation for the single black mom. Having your son watch Sesame Street or any of the PBS programs are helpful; reading begins with the understanding of the basic vowels of A-E-I-O-U. I sang the vowel song to my son every time I changed his diaper. As a toddler, my son had his flash cards I purchased from the dollar store that was held together by a shower curtain ring. I punched a hole through every card and put the cards on the ring. When my son and I went out – my son had his cards. I will also share with you that my son was Montessori schooled for Pre Kindergarten. This model of education is very unique and wonderful and as really set the foundation for my son's uniqueness that has prevailed in his learning years in public education.

Let's back up a minute... From toddler to teen your son should always leave the house with a small bag of something to amuse himself. My son reminded me of Felix the Cat because before we left the house – he always had his bag of 'tricks' ready to go. In my son's bag were a few books, simple toys and a snack. Too many times I see black moms bring their children out of the house with nothing to keep the children amused and nourished. And the children are expected to behave! Give your son his bag to keep him amused and educate him – you will see the difference in his behavior and aptitude!

One More Thing... The Dollar Store is my best friend. I can find the world in there. You can find tons of educational materials to stimulate your son's early learning at an affordable price. Puzzles, workbooks and crafts are all found at the Dollar Store!

An early reader is a strong reader. I read to my son while he was in my belly. Once he was born I read to him every night before bed. My son had favorite storybooks. Before he could talk, my son knew which stories he wanted me to read to him because he could recognize the cover of his favorite books. My son was reading by age three and that is because at home my son witnessed me reading all the time. I learned how to read at an early age because my mother is an avid reader and she still is today.

My son loves TV but I did monitor what he watched; I censored the violence, sex and length of time my son watched TV. No rap videos either. My son played with educational computer games and electronic storybooks that gave him independence from me and allowed him to navigate learning on his own.

By having your son be an early strong reader will help him in school. Your son will have no problem with state assessment tests and he will be able to comprehend better. It is also good to have your son read aloud to you. This practice builds speech, projection and articulation as well as diminishes shyness. My son still reads to me and I enjoy listening to him.

Your Black Son in School.

YOU MUST HAVE A COPY OF THE GRADUATION REQUIREMENTS FROM YOUR SON'S SCHOOL DISTRICT. This document is your guide to the required classes and exams needed for your son to successfully complete all grades until graduation. You have read my views of blacks and education. Your son is going off to school and he is now going to be exposed to things you never thought of. Once out of your home – your sanctuary, your son is going to be exposed to behaviors, words and people that you really have to stay on top of as far as knowing whom, where, and what your black son is exposed to. School is an institution that has now become a business. The following points about boundaries for your black son and school are:

· Your son is in school to be educated don't rely on the school to discipline your son.

· Do not rely upon the school to be the only method for your son to be exposed to culture and social outings. Make plans to visit museums, libraries and historical sites with your son. The exposure to these places will do him a world of good as far as his behavior and expand his imagination.

· If something is an issue at your son's school or class – please come to your son's school dressed in presentable clothes. Leave the headscarf and bedroom slippers at home! Represent yourself as an adult!

*DO NOT use profanity, do not come into the school yelling and screaming and raising all kinds of hell. Let the school staff and your son witness your self-control and ability to gather all facts before making a decision. If you don't feel comfortable going to the school by yourself. Bring someone with you or see if your son's school has a listing of advocates so that one can accompany you to support you and be your second pair of eyes and ears. An advocate can and should document your meeting in writing as well.

At home – it is important that your son has a special place to do his homework and keep his schoolwork in. Having a school week evening routine in a designated place in your sanctuary keeps everything organized and your son can do his homework undistracted. Check his schoolbag everyday for notices – please do not check his bag in front of the school – give yourself and your son time by checking beforehand so you will both be ready and prepared. Communicating with your son's teacher is essential to his education. Teachers are fully aware of which student has the participating parent – The Student's whose parents participate do very well in their education experience. The kids whose parent/guardian does not participate fall through the cracks and have a more challenging time navigating the educational system.

Successful black male students and their parents/guardians treat school as a JOB; the better you do - you will be promoted. The better prepared you are, the better the learning experience will be earned. **Be prepared to work side by side with your son.** Help him study for tests by making flash cards and testing him. Review homework and get to know your son's teachers by their names.

Parent-Teacher Night is very crucial that you are present. Usually your son's school has a school calendar so that you can plan well ahead with your employer so you can be there! This meeting is more important than any hair, nail or overtime appointment! If you cannot be there – get a stand in.

Remember – your son's education is a job that you must be present for! Don't wait until there is a problem and then show up at your son's school. Be proactive, not reactive. Too many times I see parents only twice a year: the first day of school and the last! As an parent advocate, the main statement I hear from parents: "I don't have time!" If your son needs more help – get it for him. A tutor or study guides from your local bookstore are very helpful.

Talk with his teachers to find out other resources, talk to other parents for tips and advice. Education goes further than any rap or dance contest.

Remember – education saves lives. The school experience prepares your black son to interact with the world as an adult. Ask your son how his day at school went every day.

Trouble shooting can be as simple as a pair of glasses to see the blackboard better or changing his seat in the class. Your black son needs a good night sleep and breakfast in the morning in order to have a productive school day. Please remember to monitor how much TV and video games your son watches and plays during the week and keep BOTH of these activities to a minimum. As your son's education exposure grows – he will want to learn more.

From age 8 to 14 my son witnessed me obtain three college degrees: Associate's, Bachelor's and Master's. I truly believe the exposure to academia through my college classes has affected my son's own goals and dreams of attending college. You certainly do not have to do what I did but if you are in school, for your GED, trade school or college degree – PLEASE share your learning experience with your black son! Take him to your place of learning – let him be a visitor for a day. This will have a lasting impact on your son! Discuss other options with your son as far as his future. Make graduation from high school an achievement – not a game of chance.

Your black son has a world of opportunities for him to choose from. Do not let an orange jumpsuit or the street corner become one of them. Talk about college on the regular; talk about the future. **It's not if your black son will attend college, but when!**

Your black son needs your presence, time and action now more than when he was younger. He has questions and concerns he needs to share; your son needs a person he respects and trusts to communicate with = YOU! The best way to support your son's success is to work with him side by side. For example: my son's SAT preparation included on line practice questions – we did this together. If you feel you are not up to snuff with school work – *learn beside your son!*

School activities and extra-curricular activities are wonderful networking strategies for your son. Participation in such activities exposes your son to a broader range of places and people and in turn people are exposed to him. If your son is in athletics – failing grades means he is off the team until he pulls the grades up – *this decision is yours – not the coaches!* The coach has his own agenda and job security to think of.

The school environment has changed markedly over the past twenty years. Now schools are hostile with violence, sex and drugs. Our black sons are being preyed upon by teachers who are having sex with them – our children. Please talk openly and regularly with your son about his day at school! You will be surprised at what you will find out in having these conversations with your son.

Lastly – try incentives or rewards in your son's education. I used to pay my son for every book he read and gave me a full summary on. This way, my son was reading AND earning his spending money at the same time. As my son got older, the books got longer and the fees did increase, but it was worth it! My son is well read to the point of having favorite authors and he had his pocket money that he used on things he wanted in between Kwaanza and his birthday. ** *My take on incentives: there is a black man business man who is paying children to attend school and earn good grades. I say fine—black children need to feel **valued** and education is a good place to start.*

There are some outstanding teachers in the education profession. I had the blessing of having a few in my education exposure, so has my son. These people understood that to be a teacher is a calling, to educate is a gift of acceptance and understanding that requires diligence and respect. If your black son has the same blessing – embrace it. Please remember to thank that teacher and keep them posted on the successes of your black son. These teachers need the positive encouragement and it is a wonderful way to pay it forward.

Your Special Needs/Education Black Son and School.

Having done all the supportive actions to have a good and healthy pregnancy – there is still a chance your black son could have a learning disability. DO NOT PANIC!!! Everyone learns in a unique way. Please keep your faith up that your son will evolve into an intelligent and proficient black man. I have seen so many black boys in school fall through the cracks because of special education and learning disabilities. This classification is serious for the black son, these statistics confirm the severity: African American boys spend more time is special education, less time in advanced college prep courses. Black boys who entered special education, only 10% return to a regular classroom and stay there, only 27% graduate (Source: Children's Defense Fund as of May, 2006).

Here are my experiences within the education system and special education.

* Get your son officially tested – As with any test, make sure your son has plenty of rest the night before and a good breakfast the morning of the test. Children do so much better with a good

night sleep and a solid breakfast. The mind needs rest and nutrition!

* Once testing has confirmed a special needs student – get a teaching plan, do research on local resources and get an advocate!

* Maintain the same home environment that was discussed earlier: a special place in the home to do homework, structure a routine, monitor work done and establish good communication with your son's teacher. Continue to support your son at home so that his **confidence** improves and will help him in the classroom. Many disabilities are more pronounced due to lack of confidence and self-doubt.

* Look for a summer program to maintain a continuum of learning - it is so difficult for a child to start learning in the fall, stop over the summer and then start all over again in the fall.

* Understand the politics of the education system as mentioned previously, school is now a business. Districts get more money allocated from the state for children in need of special education. Special Education is quickly assigned to a child

before exhausting and exploring other causations such as diet, home environment and medical symptoms. Special Education is immediately assigned to black males more than any other ethnicity.

* With the above being said – it is imperative that you the single black mom understands the educational system and that you make your understanding known that **YOUR SON IS NOT GOING TO BE IN SPECIAL EDUCATION FOR THE REST OF HIS LIFE.** Unless your son has a more severe handicap – Special Education is not a life-long placement. I have witnessed both black and white parents work with their son's in the public school system and get their son's **out** of special education classes and into regular classes. These boys went onto graduate and go off to college and have wonderful lives. Make sure your son's schools district does plan to evolve your black son from special education to where he can work his way into a regular class – it takes hard work, diligence and courage but it can be done.

REMEMBER – The one concept that is not advertised to parents of special education: If your son is in a special education class for a learning lag, disability or handicap, it is very likely that your son is in a classroom with other special education children who have behavioral issues along with learning ones – your son will not only have his learning issue but now due to this exposure your son will develop a behavior issue as well. Too many times I have witnessed black boys with a learning issue be placed in special education now have a behavior issue as well. This result of 'inclusion' - I am a very firm believer that these classes should be separated, or have both the learning and behavior issues addressed not just one. I am also a huge fan of separating the genders for education as well – to diminish hormonal distractions – but that is another discussion!

WHAT TO DO...

Parents are on the first line of defense – if you notice your child struggling in school and all other possibilities have been ruled out – then sit down and write a letter to the school district requesting that your son be tested. In this letter please include: Your son's name, date of birth, current school, grade, class & teacher. In this letter also immediately give permission for your son to be tested. Most likely the district will send you consent forms for the testing – but the letter implements things...This letter must be sent to the school district office, make a copy and either send by certified mail or hand deliver and request that your copy of the letter be date stamped for you to keep as proof that the letter was written and sent. Get ready to also have your son examined by his pediatrician as well. Also – get ready to meet with your son's teachers, make appointments and write down their observations of your son in class.

You must use the word **'APPROPIATE'** in place of **'BEST'**. Best is a feeling and is subjected to speculation. Appropriation fits in with the mandates of the school district. The challenge of the parent is to remove feelings and emotion – navigate like a businesswoman. I say this because the schools of today act like a business. Once you are told of the outcome of these tests, get copies and then respond in accordance to the outcome of your son's testing. Special education is a myriad of bureaucracy and politics that does not have the child's best interest as the primary focus. Parents are left as last in communication and then vehemently blamed for the child's failure. Please use local resources such as mental health and nutrition consultation to help with your son's diagnosis.

Also, get an advocate or a mentor, preferably a parent who has a child assigned to special education. If your child does have a disability, he has rights and so do you as his parent. The success your black son earns as a special education student depends upon how much action and effort you the black single mother invest in his education.

Remember – A child that is in crisis is a family that is in crisis! A successful child in school is a family that has support and services and a parent who participates.

A parent must successfully navigate the hierarchy of the school your child is in. For example: If your child is having an issue in class, first speak with your son's teacher. At the beginning of school your child's teacher gave out contact information and you supplied yours as well.

Contact the teacher first, if you are not satisfied then contact the building Assistant Principal and then the Principal. Your issue may have to go as far as the Superintendent of the school district. Always put your concerns in writing; be sure to include your child's name, teacher and class and who-what-when-where and why of the issue as you know it. Make sure your information is correct. Please provide a viable method of how you can be reached and request that you would like to be contacted as soon as possible. Follow up as needed and make it a point to forgive but not forget.

Remember: Your mannerism, attire and approach will determine the success of resolving the issue. Please come to your child's school dressed as an adult, no use of profanity, yelling or screaming. Discipline your child at home – not in front of the school. If you have to, bring an advocate with you.

Education is a business; teachers are protected by union contracts, low expectations, stigmas and politics have resulted in USA students to be lacking in education strength. Students and their families are blamed and there is a chronic breakdown in communication between schools and the families they serve. Schools belong to the students and the communities, not the teachers and principals. Many non-white students can attest to experiencing teachers telling them very negative and disparaging remarks and throwing students self esteem down. Ask any student this has happened to and they can recall the name of the teacher who said the negative remark, when it was said and in what grade. These young people never forget what was said to them! These negative comments said by teachers and faculty are detrimental of the success of the black male student. Also, teacher's posses an inherent belief: black male students do not come to class prepared nor do they know the answers to questions if called upon. As a result, many teachers frequently do not engage black male students in the classroom. This behavior rebounds back to the black male having feelings of isolation, detachment, resentment resulting in the black male student, your son losing interest in attending classes and eventually drop out. My statements are supported by a Doctorate Dissertation completed by Dr. Carol Stevens of Dutchess Community College.*

*Stevens, Carol. D. , "Skating The Zones: First Semester Experiences of African-American Male Students at a Predominantly White Community College." New York University School of Education 2006.

Dr. Stevens' dissertation: "Skating the Zones: First Semester Experiences of African American Male Students at a Predominantly White Community College (2006)" encompasses the history of blacks in America and education from high school to college. Dr. Stevens' revealed points on the black male and education:

· Stereotypes that have continued to be associated with African American males are that they are criminal, overly sexual, cool and low intelligence (Celious, 2001).

· Scholars have focused on labeling the African American "problematique"

. Some have referred to black men as an 'endangered species,' evoking memories of an earlier Darwinian belief that blacks were a separate species.

* Black male students receive more non-verbal criticism from teachers than African American females or Euro American students. They also receive more mixed messages that lead to frustration and resentment (Feagin, Vera & Imani, 1996).

* Disproportionate numbers of black boys are suspended, expelled and banished to special education than their European peers (Murrell, 2000). This results in black boys falling through the cracks of the school system

and as a result, these black males drop out and are on a fast track to prison, where the vicious cycle breeds a black man who is further ostracized from society, his community and his family.

* "The Prove Them Wrong Syndrome" is the response to society's perception of 'Black Maleness'. Even after achieving success, black men must overcome negative stereotypes (Smiles, 2002).

* The corporate media is responsible for exposing and promoting the negative images. Rap music is a billion dollar industry and **whites** have become the biggest consumers of Rap music.

* **Very few, if any black males can attribute high school guidance as a solid source of career direction and education support.**

* Many black males who are pursuing higher education often find themselves being the only men of color in the room, and they feel as though they (black men) have to represent.

* Many black students do not engage in the education assistance that is afforded to them:

speaking with the professor during office hours, tutoring and class evaluations.

* Professors and teachers alike carry the inherent action of not calling on or engaging black male students in class for fear of them not having the answer or not knowing the work.

* While white families educated their sons, black families educated their daughters.

Remember the old saying: "I RAISED my daughters, I LOVE my sons!" – Well, don't let this be you! RAISE YOUR BLACK SON – Have boundaries, expectations and hold your black son accountable!

What all of the above does to the black male student is alienate him and segregate him further in an already segregated environment. The black male student has to assess his white teachers/professors and obtain a common ground of trust before teaching/learning can begin. The black male student is often 'cool', aloof in mannerism; this is a **defense mechanism** used to protect the black male from being embarrassed, emotionally hurt or targeted. The black male also has the feeling of 'having to represent' to his peers – balancing his black identity in a predominately white influenced world of education without 'selling out' or 'acting white' to his fellow black peers which would only further alienate him in an already segregated society. All of the above is a tremendous wall that can be an obstruction to the black man in obtaining an education in America.

Everyone wants to belong and have a sense of belonging. Take Dr. Seuss and those Sneeches with and without the stars on their bellies! The black male is asked to go into a building (school, college) for several hours a day and learn among those who hold him in low regard. This is almost impossible for the black male who is unsupported in the home. Education, the concept of learning is humbling and requires a person to be **vulnerable** in order for learning to occur. Put this black male in a building with teachers/professors, his peers and that also include the opposite sex and the expectation is success? How hypocritical! Some black males can navigate this environment only if he has a very supportive forum waiting for him outside of this environment. This support must constantly engage in praise, active listening, advocacy, active involvement and patience; **many black boys and young men don't have this in their lives**.

The Educational System in America is not diversified enough to be aware of the above, the black male student is then categorized as being 'standoffish,' 'independent,' and 'not following the group.'

Education is serious, teachers and school staff should undergo a psychological evaluation every three years of employment and teachers and school staff should take an oath similar to the Physician's Hippocratic Oath. This is just how serious and how far reaching education impacts a young black son. One misguided teacher, principal or guidance counselor making a derogatory statement to your black son can have a life- long impact. I am encountering this very scenario today – many young people I speak with tell me of their own incident where a faculty member told them that they should settle for a menial job and not look into college or vocational school because they can't do it.

In Conclusion-Education is a business that is not benefiting our black sons!

Our black sons have challenges in the learning arena. Your college bound black son will find out that there are not as many scholarships focused on males as there are for females. The lament is always that there are more females in college than males. There are more support programs in place for college bound females than males. If there were more scholarship opportunities for males who are college bound – there is a strong likelihood that more males would be in college. Males who are 18 must also register with Selective Services in order to obtain Federal Aid for college – this is a definite deterrent for males who want to attend college but do not want to sign up. There is absolutely nothing wrong in wanting to serve the USA in the armed services.

Historically, blacks were treated inferiorly in the armed services and this also deters black males from registering. Juvenile Delinquencies that are of court record are sealed and should not deter a young black man from seeking higher education.

Chapter Six

A Good Diet = A Healthy Boy = A Strong King

Boys like to eat! Nutrition is vital for the development of both mind and body – it is very difficult to concentrate when you are hungry or thirsty. Food is another serious aspect of your black son's life. Microwaves have changed the family dinning dynamics: Now the microwave produces meals in minutes. As a result of just pushing a button many children are left at home with the microwave preset to heat up dinner. The microwave has freed Mama from the kitchen and a nurturing meal was also lost. We have made a huge sacrifice for time.

A family that eats together maintains a bond of communication and intimacy. My son and I are very busy people – but we do manage to eat at least one meal together every day. I am against fast foods as a constant meal provider – I don't care if McDonalds accepts food stamps! Fast foods are expensive and can be a danger to health as they contain high levels of sodium, fats and cholesterol.

Historically, it is very important that blacks watch their diet as we are predisposed to diabetes, hypertension and obesity. For your son – leave out soda, mayonnaise, candy, white bread, fried foods and all snacks that can sit on the shelf for months at a time! I have also encountered black mothers who restrict their child's diet to match their own belief and they use special light bulbs, goat's milk and many other extraneous things. I say more power to them if they have the time and money.

Your black son needs to make up his own mind about vegan/vegetarian diets the same way as ear piercing. Until adulthood, your son needs a ton of vitamins, minerals, folic acid and a healthy balance of fats and sugars. Please maintain your son's visits and check-ups with his pediatrician and dentist. As far as vitamins, your son can use a chewable vitamin that is recommended by his pediatrician, I used one with fluoride so that my son's teeth grew strong. Your son also needs whole grains and vegetables daily. Snacks can be fun and healthy – remember that. Juices are so much better than sodas. Watch dairy products as your son maybe lactose intolerant. Asthmatics or a person with seasonal allergies should also watch dairy intake because dairy intake does cause an increase of the production of phlegm = making your son more congested than he already is.

Baby Boy Needs Stimulation!

Neuro (nerve) development is found all over our bodies. When someone tells you: "You got a lot of nerve!" You really do! From fetal development in your womb, your son needs all of his nerves to be strong and functioning. Not only are his nerves present at birth; they need to be stimulated as well.

Nutrition as discussed above is very helpful as your son is growing at a rapid rate. Exercise also stimulates the muscles and nerves throughout the body. Boys like to run, jump and climb! Keeping him healthy means providing the proper stimulation from infancy through adulthood. Keeping your baby in the crib all day on his back is not proper brain or body stimulation, your toddler son needs to move and explore as he is getting used to his limbs and eye-hand coordination. Music, educational toys and shows will stimulate your black son's brain – an organ that is made up of millions of nerves. You may not 'see' the results but you will notice them in his behavior. It is important that you do censure what your black son is watching. Violent video games, music videos and movies have to be censured and appropriate. If you are going to the movies – please get a sitter for your young son – don't bring him. You many not think he does not understand because he is so little – but don't take the chance – the loud noises are just not suitable for young ears.

Newborns are learning their new environment outside the womb: smells, voices, sounds (including his own) lights, temperatures, everything. Stimulate your infant black son by singing and reading to him. Let him sleep in an environment that has some noise – not complete silence. As your son goes off to pre-school neuro stimulate your school aged black son with flashcards, board games (Concentration, Picture Bingo, etc). The biggest difference between my generation and my son's generation is technology. Children of yesterday (me) relied upon eye-hand games and activities that required multi-tasking, problem solving and listening.

Today's generation relies on technology that is eye – hand held and super fast – usually skipping several steps and arriving at the end result with little or no analytical thought process in between! Today's generation is all about technology – computers. Computers do over 20 functions in one keystroke. As a result of this work being done outside of the brain, today's generation is stimulated differently and their ability to multitask, problem solve and listen is greatly diminished. **PLEASE DO NOT RELY UPON TELEVISON SHOWS AND VIDEO GAMES TO PARENT AND STIMULATE YOUR BLACK SON!!!**

Sure – it is great to let your son explore computerized educational games in order to learn how to operate a computer and to watch an educational program on television, but it is also good to let your son do manual work that requires **listening** as well as eye-hand coordination.

There are ways to neuro-stimulate your black son in today's technology that will develop his mind and how he processes critical thinking:

* Play board games with your son. This teaches concentration, eye- hand coordination and analytical thinking. Your son will be multitasking with the dice (counting), moving his man (concentration) and trying to win! (setting goals in the immediate future) as well as strategizing! Picture Bingo, Trouble, Sorry and Scrabble are great board games to play.

* A good card game is also excellent: Old Maid, UNO, Go Fish are favorites – also when he is older – teach him Spades so he beat the pants off a few girls!

* Give your son a command to do – now stack the commands – meaning – give more than one command to do and ask him to do it in the order you gave it to him.

* Read to your son and then ask him to summarize what you read to him. Math problems are also excellent to have your son do verbally to hone up on his listening skills.

* Play 'I Spy' in the house or outside. Spot something and then have your son find it – you can advance the game by having him spell the things you spy as well.

* Get your black son involved physically: swimming, karate or playing a musical instrument are excellent activities that will benefit your black son in his future. Swimming is a MUST. This builds confidence and is an excellent skill to have in case your son is near water. I had my son swimming since he was a toddler now he surfs!

Do's and Don'ts (I had to say it!).

Boys will be boys – they love things that go fast, explode and are slimy. Do not stifle your son's curiosity. Give your black son supervision to explore. Let your son play with dolls and tea sets – he will play with them in school with other children. Do not gender separate toys from your black son. Your son is not gay if he plays with dolls and tea sets. Please do not discriminate.

- **Do** allow your son to have a special toy that he plays with, sleeps with and takes everywhere. - Do not allow uncensored music and videos to be shown to your black son.

- **Do not** allow your black son to speak slang, or speak in phonetic mispronunciations, recite rap songs that are filled with profanity and derogatory remarks.

- **Do** introduce your black son to a wide range of music, art and dance. Jazz, Rock, Country and Classical music are all wonderful in their unique way – introduce your son to them and let him grow. If your son shows athletic talent – terrific! Just make it very clear that in all activities: art, music and athletics – your son will also learn how to read, write and do math! None of these extra talents are to replace the basic skills or reading, writing and mathematics! Take your son to plays and concerts and teach him how to behave and conduct himself out in public.

Remember – your son watches how *you* behave – so be a sound role model. The earlier your son is exposed to going out to restaurants, museums, etc, the better his behavior will be and his exposure to this type of stimulation with the proper support from you – your son will be charming and well behaved to the point that you look forward to going out together!

***Part of this exposure is learning the proper etiquette: Table manners, being a gentleman and holding the door, etc. These skills your black son takes with him for life and the early exposure makes all of this effortless and quite natural.

Mamma's Nutrition & Stimulation – Yes You Can!

What goes for your son as far as eating and brain stimulation also applies for you! Eating healthy, vitamins and exercising are vital to you being the best single mom you can be! Taking care of yourself keeps you mentally and physically fit to face the challenges of single parenting. Your health should not take away from your son's childhood experience!

Try recipes in cooking. There are creative ways to buy some take out and combine it with what you cooked at home to make a great meal. Take time to pumice your feet, lotion up and keep your hair groomed! So many times I get wonderful compliments from women about my hair. I always reply with the fact that I take vitamins for my hair to grow and I eat hair growing foods. You can't keep slapping weave tracks, relaxer chemicals and braids in your hair – you have to eat hair growing foods for your hair to be healthy. Call a few girlfriends over and give each other facials! Just because you are a single mom does not mean you have to look busted!

Want to feel better? DRINK MORE WATER! & GET SOME MORE SLEEP!!!! Grab you Mommy Mentor and talk out your feelings. The other option for you is to get a therapist.

There is nothing wrong in having a therapist to talk out your feelings and move on with your life!

Single parenting is very stressful. This stress can cause resentment, anger, fatigue, depression and more that can have a lasting and negative effect on you and your black son's life. Think about yourself in your black son's eyes. Don't let your black son grow up thinking that all black women are dysfunctional, mentally riddled with issues and are un-kept and unproductive. Your dysfunctions will become your son's dysfunctions and that is no inheritance to give to anyone!

As a black single mother – your attire, dress and attitude must reflect grace, maturity and boundaries. Dressing like a 17 year old is not you. Even if you are a 17 year old mother, dress like an adult – you are one now. Ghetto fabulous is not for you either! Cover up those stretch marks and tattoos! Replace loud and ostentatious fashions with practicality and class.

Remember – Queens do not dress like the court jester!

Let's take the first step in letting go of the past... An excerpt from "O, The Magazine" July 2006 by Martha Beck:

Storytelling to shed light OK; obsessing aloud to gain pity not healthy   Concentrate on the here and now instead of painful problems of past   You can't redo the past, but you can toss out old, false ideas Working scared, confused or embarrassed toward goals is OK By Martha Beck **(Oprah.com)** –

Poignant, tragic, funny, outrageous --most of us have at least one story we tell (and retell) to explain our emotional bruises. But there's a big difference between understanding the past and being stuck in it. Self-pity, a dominant characteristic of sociopaths, is also the characteristic that differentiates heroic storytelling from psychological rumination. When you talk about your experiences to shed light, you may feel wrenching pain, grief, anger, or shame. Your audience may pity you, but not because you want them to. Obsessing aloud, on the other hand, is a way of fishing for pity, a means of extorting attention. Healthy people instinctively resist this strategy. When you grieve, they will yearn to comfort you. When you demand pity, they will yearn to smack you. All day, I've been telling stories to evoke my own pity, and it's working. Partly. The unhealthy part of me, the world- class codependent, is just mesmerized. "Oh," she cries, "you poor darling! Tell me that sad story again -- the first 400 times didn't do it justice!" The healthy part of me finds this annoying: "Oh, for God's sake," she says, rolling her eyes. "Could we please stop the drama and get on with our life?" The healthy part of me is such a heartless bitch. On the other hand, she's got a point. Compulsively examining my stories never works for me. I keep sinking into sorrow (self-inflicted though it is) until it occurs to me that I will drown unless I can drag myself out. This can be difficult, but after decades of practice, I've created a sort of verbal tree limb I can grab in a pinch: *Am I presently learning the truth about my life's work?* If this sentence sounds a little vague, that's because it's actually a mnemonic code. Each phrase reminds me of a concept that helps me escape the marsh: being present, learning continuously, seeking truth, and committing my energy to my real life's work.

Become present I just met with a client I'll call Kristin, an energetic self-pitier. We were discussing her desire for a promotion when her gaze dropped and her voice took on a

timbre both sorrowful and weirdly practiced, as though
she were reciting a very depressing Pledge of Allegiance.
"You know," Kristin said, her eyes welling up, "my mother
never let me talk back to her, never really listened to me."
Her chest began to heave. "My therapist says she may as
well have been deaf." She dissolved into tears. "Oh," I said.
"So, are you going to ask for that promotion?" "She never
listened!" Kristin repeated, sobbing, her hand on her neck.
"My astrologer says it totally blocked my throat chakra!"
"Kristin," I said, "Look at me, please." She didn't want to. I
insisted. "How many fingers am I holding up?" Reluctantly,
like a dog dropping a stolen ham, Kristin raised her eyes
and looked. "Three," she said. Her tears dried up. She
seemed disappointed. The story-fondling thing had been
going so well. "Kristin, can you see that your mother isn't
here? Can you hear that you are able to speak? You're a
full-grown woman, with a functioning larynx, who wants a
promotion. Full stop." I call this anchoring, establishing a
simple, physical, factual connection with present reality.
Try it for yourself, right now. Look around you. Listen.
Touch your hair, the floor, this page. Whatever happened
10 years ago, whatever happened 10 minutes ago, is not
your present concern. Neither is what will happen in

another 10 years, another 10 minutes. This moment is all you have to worry about. Narrowing your attention to this point is your reconnection with solid ground.

Never stop learning Getting bogged down in old stories stops the flow of learning by censoring our perceptions, making us functionally deaf and blind to new information. Once the replay button gets pushed, we no longer form new ideas or conclusions -- the old ones are so cozy. But becoming present puts us back in reality, where we can rigorously fact-check our own tales. Try dredging up one of your favorite stories --maybe a classic like "I'm not good enough." Treat it as a hypothesis. Research it. Is there any evidence that contradicts it? Have you ever, in any way, even for an instant, been good enough? You may need to ask someone for coaching at first. Evidence that contradicts your hypothesis will be hard for you to see, while to an objective observer, it's obvious ("Well, you're good enough for me, your dog, and everyone down at the bingo hall, you dumb cluck"). However you get to it, the moment you absorb a fact that disproves your hypothesis, you're half out of the mire.

Insist on the truth Whatever terrible things may have happened to you, only one thing allows them to damage your core self, and that is continued belief in them. Kristin's mother may have been Stalin in a bra, but by the time Kristin got to my office, what was silencing her was the conviction she'd formed during interactions with Mom: "It's no good to speak up; no one will ever hear me." Kristin couldn't redo her past, but she could change that belief. In fact, the loop she replayed in her head was the one thing standing in her way, since evidence disconfirming her hypothesis was everywhere. Lots of people listened to Kristin. Once she acknowledged that, she couldn't be a tiny victim, waiting haplessly for her chakras to open. She was just a woman with a scary job to do. I know how much this realization bummed her out; it always bums me out. But then, it's also the doorway to freedom.

Put all your energy into your life's work The moment you lift your gaze from your old stories, you'll see your life's work. I don't mean a gilt-edged proclamation from God, describing every step you are to take for the rest of your existence. I mean the next step, which is usually very small: Ask for the promotion. Pick up the kids. Take a nap. Then take the step that comes after that. From time to time, as you continue along, a Big Dream will coalesce out of the swamp fog. The way forward is to shake the quicksand off your feet and take one small step toward that dream. Trust me, it will be all you can do. Taking things step-by-step means working -- working hard, working scared, working through confusion and embarrassment and failure. I've met many people the world thinks of as "lucky," and all of them operate this way. I've come to think that the main purpose of rumination is work avoidance. Dwelling endlessly on the past keeps us from the wild, exhausting, terrifying tasks that create our right lives. When I become a little more ruthless with myself and a lot more present in what I have to do, I see that writing a humble column is my next step -- and I have writer's block. I'd love to enter therapy and figure out why, but I don't have that kind of time. Instead, I'll focus on a saying from the Ojibwa tradition, one that deserves the attention I customarily lavish on my problems: *Sometimes I go about pitying myself, and all the while I am being carried on great winds across the sky. By Martha Beck from "O, The Oprah Magazine," July 2006*

LET GO OF THE PAST – HOPEFULLY THE ABOVE ARTICLE TARGETS SOME OF THESE AREAS FOR YOU – LEAVE THE PAST – GROW FROM IT – BUT MOVE ON. YOU WILL BE HEALTHIER AND HAPPIER AND SO WILL YOUR BLACK SON.

For you single black mama – you can stimulate yourself in a happy and self-loving manner! Vibrators, Girl's Night Out, African Dance Classes, Pliates and Yoga are all good methods of self-love! Buy yourself flowers; take yourself out to your favorite restaurant. There are many books to read and degrees to obtain! Stimulation is NOT drugs, alcohol or promiscuous sex! Build your temple for God's reward! Take care of your body! Prayer, positive affirmations and meditations are great methods of self-love. I firmly believe that schools should start the day with positive affirmations and mediations for the students.

Prayer is just not for when you are in trouble – prayer is also in good times, in times of awareness and for spiritual growth. Meditation slows and calms the mind down, allowing for awareness and enlightenment to occur. Black single moms – you must be in love with yourself before anyone else can love you. Here are my examples of loving you:

   * When you love you – You will not let anyone physically, verbally or mentally abuse you.

   * When you love you – You will treat your body as the temple for God's presence, you will abstain from abusing drugs (of any kind) and alcohol.

   * When you love you- You will take care of your body and not get fat, grungy, and trendy.

   * When you love you – You possess boundaries that none will trespass.

   * When you love you – you will have a belief of self sufficiency – you will have your home stocked and not have to borrow from your neighbor, family or friends. "God helps those who help themselves."

   * When you love you – you will see your son as an extension of yourself and a gift from God – you will let no

one mess with your son! To do so is messing with you and that is just not acceptable!

* When you love you – you will be in control of your relationships and you will be able to let go of people who are not really friends they claim to be, you will let go of men who are not feeding your mind & your heart.

* When you love you – You will understand that lust is temporary and love is patience and lasting. You will understand the power of sex and the power of your vagina/womb.

* When you love you – You will be both male and female – you will understand that being a man in this world is temporary – Until God puts a man in your path – you are first and foremost a woman – a Queen.

* When you love you – You will carry yourself with grace, manners and humility. Your faith is your armor, your son is your strength and God is the reason you live. Through Him all things are possible.

* When you love you – You let the world see you treasure your son wear your pride of motherhood, there is no shame, no regret or remorse.

Chapter Seven

Adolescence

Be a Leader – Not a Follower.

Your black son is going through a challenging time – adolescence. This Right of Passage is going to be tough, ugly and downright hard! Your son and the world he goes into everyday will test you time and time again, there will be peaks of joy and success and there will be valleys of darkness and uncertainty. Your son is a leader by the years of self-esteem building you have put into him from birth along with boundaries. Being aware of whom he hangs out with, allowing your black son and his friends to hang out at your house with your supervision, being a parental presence at your son's schools, modeling your own awareness and behavior of a leader for your son – all of these things develop a leader.

Too many times I have witnessed single black moms make a critical mistake: leaving your black son on auto parent while you work is a huge no-no. I have seen two parent homes with both parents working very long hours of overtime and the other parent works a long way from home, resulting in having to leave very early in the morning and returning home very late – all for big dollars of income, trophy home and lifestyle. This couple sacrificed their children for their own desires of material possessions. Their children were left on their own as latch key kids for hours on end – this resulted in teen pregnancy, deviant behavior, school drop-out and drug use. Make the sacrifice as a single parent – do not assume your son can be left at home alone always!

The second mistake I witness parents make: Their son is at home with them – its eleven o'clock on a week night – the door bell rings and it's the son's friends. Now your son wants to go out with his friends at eleven o'clock at night on a school night to nowhere. You let him go in his slippers because he says he is coming right back. 3:30 AM your phone rings – it's the police and your son is now in jail – he was arrested with his 'friends' on a weapons charge, drug possession and resisting arrest. The gun and cocaine was found in the car your son was riding in; the 'friends' all said the gun and drugs belong to your son. Your son is prosecuted and sentenced to 15 years – with no parole until eight years have been served. All of this occurred because you had no boundaries to tell your son to stay his ass at home and NO – his friends CANNOT come to your home at 11PM at night! Leaders are able to tell their friends that he has boundaries to uphold. Leaders are able to make decisions that do not place them at risk. **Leaders are not afraid of saying no.**

Your black son's identity and individuality are with him from birth. As an adolescent do not let your son loose his identity and individuality to anyone – not even to you. Being liked is not as important as being smart!

I went to a seminar very early in my social work education and I came across a display table that was set up with materials for adolescents and self esteem building. There were laminated cards that a young boy or girl could put in their wallet or bag. I read this card and then I grabbed a handful. I gave my son one to keep in his wallet and then I gave out some to his friends:

FRONT OF CARD	BACK OF CARD
Key Questions	**Positive Values**
Is this a risky situation?	Caring
Am I being pressured?	Equality & Social Justice
How would my parent(s)	Integrity
feel about this?	Honesty
Is this consistent with my values?	Responsibility
What effect will this have on	Restraint
my future?	
What other choices do I have?	

These values are important to me and my relationship with others.
YOUR SON THEN SIGNS THE BOTTOM OF THIS CARD
AND DATES IT.
WWW.SEARCH-INSTITUTE.ORG

My son kept this laminated card in his wallet for a long time – when I gave him his card we talked about the meaning of the card and its function in his wallet – a constant reminder **to think before acting** – Be a leader. Having a wallet is important for a young black man – your son needs his identification with him at all times. Having identification establishes your son as a person with an origin and a place of rest. I really can't stand seeing blacks walk out of their home without a wallet or identification, this is dangerous and the police immediately assume criminal intent when encountering the black male without identification. Giving your son a wallet in the middle school also helps build responsibility. Sure someone will try to steal his wallet and he may lose it a few times and this will pass. Your black son will learn not to flash his wallet and to respect the contents – his money and identification. Identification is vital to the black son – identification states a belonging to someone and someplace.

Show You Care – Listen.

Listening is a powerful skill that many do not have. To listen to your black son is a powerful self-esteem building tool that will forge a bond between you and your son that will last a lifetime. You son's communication of his needs, concerns and actions to you is very important in the mother-son relationship. The most common desire of a human being is to be *heard.* The dialogue between you and your son is the core of your relationship. By listening to your black son he will come to you again and again as a resource, as a trustworthy person to respect. Your listening has opened up a path of communication that is fortified with trust, respect and love.

Monique was featured in Essence Magazine September 2008. Monique spoke openly about being molested as a child by a family member. When she went to her family and told them – they would not listen nor did they believe her. How devastating that had to be: A child goes to her parents and tells them someone has molested her and she is not validated, not supported, not helped! **It may be painful but please listen to your son if he comes to you and tells you something has happened to him!** To ignore and deny in this communication will result in your son being scared for life and will affect his future relationships and how he communicates! This is not about you; this is about your black son. If you don't listen to him, neither will the world – YOU are his world!

Guess what? By you modeling being a good listener to your black son – he will in turn becomes a good listener and he will also ask questions that are attending and sincere. I absolutely love it when my son asks me: "How was your day?" I don't care how many times I have heard it I get angry just the same as if I heard it for the first time. Black men saying: "Well, that boy got into trouble because there was not any male presence in the home." This makes me want to scream! Having a man in the house **does not** mean all problems are solved, it **does not** mean your son will not encounter any problems. If that mom were listening, she could have begun taking action to help her son steer away from trouble! No one likes to be preached to - everyone wants to be heard, **especially** adolescents and teens.

Listening to society, single mothers hear all the time the statement I mentioned above on a child's deviant behavior is due to being raised by a single parent and not having a male presence in the home. As I said this constant misconception is now being brought to the light. Dr. Michael Lamb a psychology professor at the University of Cambridge England states: "Yes, there is a risk, but it is not a risk inherent in the single-parent family per se. You can't assume that every child raised by a single parent is going to have difficulties. The majority don't." Societal concerns were driven by cultural assumptions which remains fixated that children do better in two parent homes. Dr. Lamb states: "The evidence, on the whole, hasn't supported that, but the beliefs have persisted in society."*

What I have always said to anyone who has came forward to me and judged me because I am a single parent is that I made the choice to raise my son in a home with one happy parent as opposed to being in a home with two miserable parents. Dr. Lamb offers this view: "Children do better if they have a good relationship with the in-home parent, as well as if the parents have low conflict. What's important is not whether they (children) are raised by one or two parents. It is how good is the relationship with the parent, how much support they're (children) getting from that parent and how harmonious is the environment."*

I have also heard so many times that boys need their fathers the way girls need their mothers in child rearing. Dr. Tim Biblarz a sociologist of the University of Southern California disagrees with the above statement. Dr. Biblarz states: "I can tell you there's almost no evidence supporting that. For a variety of reasons, children who grow up with single fathers for example are at higher risk than those who grow up with single mothers for either sex."*

Unfortunately, this belief has been long standing in society and the belief is so strong that it pushes black women into having a man in their home and life that is abusive, inappropriate with drug use or an under achiever. **Your black son does not need this.** This societal belief is detrimental to the black man as a child (he witnesses the inappropriate man in his sanctuary; the black son is witness to violence and destructive behaviors) and the black woman; his mother as it strongly implies that the black mother is **not** enough (diminishes her importance) in parenting and family.

What my book is strongly supporting is that your black son be supported in his upbringing with boundaries, parental presence, diligence and values so that your black son can become the best man, the king that he is capable of becoming. Support your son in his abilities like an Olympic Gold Medalist; years of practice and training. If your son shows ability, then support him and support him in the basic educational needs so that your black son will be competitive in any arena. **The black mother who is accountable, participating in her black son's life in all areas and is a focused parent is enough for the black son and she has every ability to be successful in raising her black son to be a man who is positive, productive and proactive in his life and the world.**

*Drs. Lamb and Biblarz are quoted from: Jayson, Sharon, "Single Moms & Successful Sons: New research conflicts with common beliefs. Gannett News Service. September 21, 2008. www.PoughkeepsieJournal.com.Retrieved September 21, 2008.

Listening is not taught in the schools but it is constantly demanded. Listening is part of leadership and a skill that every black man needs. When one listens, much is revealed as opposed to talking constantly. Historically, our ancestors were great listeners: so many times valuable information was obtained by a black house worker who remained silent; almost invisible and listened to conversations being held by whites. Everything from stock tips to real estate know-how to people of influence information was garnered and those black ancestors who listened became prosperous.

A current example, Michael Jackson befriended Paul McCartney many years ago and Paul gave Michael advice on how to really succeed in the music business (own the songs that were written—by anyone) and Michael listened. Mr. Jackson lives off of royalty payments for the songs that he owns. If Mr. Jackson did not listen and continued to talk – he would have missed valuable information. Train your son to be a listener! YOU be a listener to your black son!

Mental Health and the Black Son.

Observation is the second attribute to listening – your black son may have a mental health issue that needs help – don't be in denial. Don't be afraid to get help – if you wait, the court judge will appoint the needed mental health services for your son. Don't let the issue get that far. Mental health is detrimental in blacks due to poor diagnosing, denial and lack of knowledge. Blacks get the poorest medical care in the United States. *It's no fault of anyone – your son has two sets of genes – so leave the blaming the out.* Now is the time for you to step up your advocating and support of your black son. Be aggressive and assertive in your son's therapist care and medical intervention. An untreated mental health issue can lead to drug/alcohol use, violence, police intervention and even incarceration.

The advancement of medical technology today demands your black son have the best care and that you give his situation your utmost attention and advocacy. In adolescence, teens experience more depression, anger and stress due to peer pressure, gangs, sex and violence. Be hyper-observant and do not forget to sit down with your son and make up some positive affirmations for him to use. Also use "I love you", "You are important to me" and "You can be anything you want to be." **You are your son's cheering squad of one and you have got to be loud enough for thousands!**

Utilize your local mental health department as a resource. Your search and obtaining a mental health provider is the same approach as securing a pediatrician.

As the result of 400 years of slavery, blacks have inherited Post **Traumatic Slavery Disorder** (PTSD), stress and many consider blacks to be 'damaged goods' because of this legacy (which has not been given to any other race) and transference of PTSD/stress through the **womb**. There has never been any mass therapy session after slavery blacks have *never* recovered from 400 years of gross trauma. The DSM IV (Diagnostic Statistical Manual) – the bible of psychology is *not culturally diverse* to acknowledge blacks and the lack of healing from 400 years of slavery in the Unites States of America.

The Angry Black Young Man.

There is another area of mental health that I would also like to discuss: **Anger**. For blacks anger is faced on a daily basis, simply for existing. This awareness of race is transferred through the womb; blacks have the ability of analyzing just who is a racist and who is not. This assessment ability also brings anger. 400 years of oppression in the worst forms imaginable, human torture and disfigurement, emotional trauma and socioeconomic oppression; there have to be anger. This anger has been inherited through the womb. So many times I have witnessed anger in our young black children. This anger comes at any time and is usually the result of frustration— an inner frustration. Anger that is left unaddressed results in violence in our black youth.

This anger is not deviant behavior, but the result of enduring racism. Remember, blacks experience a different life in a community—just by being what God made them— BLACK! To go out into the world is to face constant scrutiny, low expectation, negative stigmas and lack of respect. This anger is simply a defense mechanism as the result of being constantly exposed to the above for over 400 years.

Your son will display anger—you have to recognize this and help him understand this feeling; when it comes upon him he must learn how to control this anger and redirect it to another action—a positive one. This anger may be directed at you because you are supporting boundaries and rules. It is important for you to explain to your son that you are supporting these boundaries and rules to save his life. This is also why it is so important for you and your son to have that high level of trust that has been mentioned throughout this book.

Anger left unaddressed and unidentified by a parent results in a young man who self medicates with drugs, risky behavior and violent tendencies—why? Your black son cannot explain what is happening to him and WHY; he is still a youth. I have seen many black young men, from good homes, two parent homes are pot heads, into thrill dangerous behaviors and commit random acts of violence because this anger is not identified and addressed. Once the anger is addressed and support is given—a black man's life is saved. The tentacles of slavery extend well beyond the 400 years our ancestors have endured.

If there are any doubts, Lay My Burden Down. By Dr. Alan F. Poussaint and Amy Alexander discuss the epidemic of blacks and suicide in their book published in 2000. Unaddressed mental anguish often leads to depression, suicide, violent behaviors that I have already discussed. Black Pain: It Looks Like We Are Not Hurting. By Terrie Williams is a current book that also addresses black mental health. Please, be aware of any signs of mental distress your son may exhibit and please get help for your son—it may save his life.

IF YOUR BLACK SON DISPLAYS BOUTS OF ANGER, ADDRESS IT IMMEDIATELY!

An Angry Black Man is Never A King!

Mentoring.

Ok – it's just you and your son – having a mentor is a great thing and a true blessing. A sincere, professional male presence, black or white is a wonderful attribute in your son's life. Make sure you set up boundaries and screen your son's mentor carefully. Big Brother – Big Sister is a wonderful agency and they carefully screen mentors. I am a firm believer that we all need mentors in all stages in our lives. We don't know everything and it is such a blessing to have guidance along the way.

Remember – Your son's mentor is not his father. Your son's mentor is not Santa either. Maintain boundaries and keep listening/observing your son.

Mentoring can help the single mother. A mentor can provide guidance, support and encouragement with the goal of supporting the development of your son to have healthy family and social relationships and be productively involved in their communities (Gambone, Conell, Klem, Sipe & Bridges, 2002).*

All *of this can be done with just four hours a month.*
Research shows that when mentoring programs are
implemented well, mentoring is an effective way to help
youth, who lack either stable relationships or positive role
models in their lives improve academic achievement, build
a stronger sense of self worth, improve relationships with
parents and other adults and decrease the likelihood of
negative behaviors (Jucovy, 2003).**

*Gambone, Conell, Klem, Sipe & Bridges, 2002. "The Mentoring Tool
Kit Resources for Developing Programs for Incarcerated Youth."
National Evaluation and Technical Assistance Center for the Education
of Children and Youth Who Are Neglected, Delinquent, or At Risk.
U.S. Department of Education. Retrieved June 2008.
**Jucovy, Linda. —Amachi: Mentoring Children of Prisoners in
Philadelphia.‖ June 2003. Retrieved June 2008.

What Is My Role as a Mentor?

It seems simple at first, the notion of being a mentor:
someone who spends time with a young person. But once
you are in the mentor role, you may find yourself in
situations where you are uncertain about your part in the
relationship. Is it appropriate to provide discipline when
she's out of line? What if I suspect he is experiencing
trouble at home—what is my responsibility? How can I
have the most positive impact on my mentee? There is no
one answer concerning what your role is or is not. If you
are involved in a formal mentoring program, the staff may

be able to provide clearer direction for you based on the program's rules and expectations. In general, here are some basic guidelines to help you determine your role with your mentee:

YOU ARE . . . . . . a friend. Like peer friendships, mentors and mentees do things together that are fun and engaging. They support each other both in good times and in tough times. They teach each hard conversations about concerns they have, asking the right questions at the right time. By being a good listener and engaging in authentic conversations with your mentee, you are helping him develop important life skills. . . .

A role model. You are expected to set a good example to the mentee for how to live your life. This is not the same as being perfect. Rather, it is about acknowledging your imperfections and sharing your strengths. It is also about advocating for your mentee when dangers to his physical or emotional well-being are present. . . .

A confidant. Building a close relationship with your mentee will help her build better relationships with others in his life as well, such as parents and peers. In the process, your mentee may tell you things he does not feel comfortable telling anyone else. Sometimes he may tell you about his hopes, dreams, or insecurities. Other times he may reveal mistakes he has made. Unless your mentee is in trouble and needs outside help, try to keep his private comments between the two of you. Your role is to be supportive of your mentee as a person with potential, regardless of the kinds of actions or attitudes he confides in you. . . .

A nurturer of possibilities. Your role is to see the gifts and strengths of your mentee and help him flourish personally. You should help your mentee channel his gifts toward actions that make him a resource to others in his family, neighborhood, school, or community.

YOU ARE NOT . . . . . .
A mentor to the family. In fact, some mentoring programs intentionally limit contact between mentors and parents. Your role is to provide special attention to your mentee. While getting acquainted with parents, caregivers, and siblings can be helpful to understanding your mentee and his situation, your energy and attention should be focused on providing support to your mentee. . . .
A social worker or doctor. If your mentee tells you about experiences or health conditions that concern you, always turn to the mentoring program staff for help. Although arming yourself with information about, say, a learning disability or abuse may help you understand your mentee better, it is not your responsibility to try to address conditions or situations that require professional help. The staff at the mentoring program may be able to find additional help for the mentee, including local information and referral services. . . .
A savior. You should not see your role in this relationship as coming in to make a young person's life better or to fix his problems. Certainly your support can help your mentee overcome hurdles. But don't forget that every young person—regardless of his circumstances—has gifts and talents that make him more than a —recipientǁ of your support. Your mentee should be treated as having much to offer to the world, because he does. Developmental Assets™ are positive factors within young people, families, communities, schools, and other settings that research has found to be important in promoting young people's development.

From *Mentoring for MeaningfulResults: Asset-Building Tips, Tools, and Activities for Youth and Adults.* Copyright © 2006 by Search InstituteSM; 800-888-7828; www.search-institute.org

Sex Talk.

It's gonna happen! Your black son is going to ask THOSE questions! From the time your son starts closing the door when he goes to the bathroom until he goes to school – he is going to ask all kinds of questions about you (girls), about him (boys) and sex.

YES – your son knows you are made up differently from him. Yes – your son will see two people kissing (on the street, in a movie or show, anywhere) and he will have questions. As your son gets older – you don't have to deal with the period – you have to deal with growth spurts, voice changes, facial hair and wet dreams (nocturnal emissions).

Hopefully, you and your son are close and you can maintain a trusted level of communication. Trust and communication are essential when talking about sex. Your son realizes he has something down there! - starting with his first erection in his diaper. Your son will touch himself as a way of curiosity. It's okay. Now it is crucial that you handle yourself and your son's sexuality/puberty awareness very carefully – if you don't, there could be emotional damage in the form of repression, avoidance and withdrawal that could affect your son as a man.

Masturbation is healthy and very natural. Some children are actually frightened about their bodies changing. Calm your son and get help - there are wonderful books at your local bookstore and library that are fun and user friendly for you and your son. Be open with your son: talking about blowjobs, penises, vaginas and feeling good are discussions you have to have with your son.

School is a huge vat of **misinformation** that your son and his peers encounter from one another – keep your son well informed – the right information comes from you. You must bone up (no pun intended!) on your sex knowledge.

It is important to talk to your son about good touching and bad touching. Pedophiles come in all shapes, sizes, races, and genders. Sexual abuse can come from family, a care provider, a teacher, a priest, etc. Talk with your son about the dangers of this and let your son's pediatrician help you. Have very clear discussions with your son about the use of protection and sex. Buy a pack of condoms and let your son practice on a banana, let him open a condom and have that experience. Planned Parenthood is not just for girls – guys can get information and free condoms there.

Discuss with your son the realities of sexuality transmitted diseases such as HIV/Aids. Let your son know that if he becomes sexually active- he can come to you and let you know. Once he is sexually active – you son's annual physical exam with his pediatrician changes to include STI testing and education.

Remember: If your son gets a girl pregnant as a teenager – he has no say in aborting or keeping that baby – the girl ultimately does. If she is younger than your son, her parents may press criminal charges of statutory rape against your son. Tell your son to practice protection is to have control – unprotected sex renders your black son powerless and could even kill him if he contracts the HIV/Aids virus.

Along with your son's sexual development comes his hygiene care: shaving, bathing, deodorant and dental care as well as treatment for acne. Support your son though this time – take him to a dermatologist for his acne, take him to the dentist for his teeth and educate your son on deodorant, men's cologne and bathing. Of course go to the dollar store for some of these items that your son can practice with inexpensively.

Your son's teeth, hair and skin care are all part of his sexuality and self esteem with the opposite sex. Any deficiencies in these areas could be harmful to your son's emotional health. His self esteem and communication skills are related to his hygiene, hair, skin and teeth. Take your son to the dentist twice a year for a cleaning and check-ups. Healthy teeth are part of the body's overall health. Slaves were examined on the auction block from their head to their toes. Any kind of dental/oral issue has to be addressed to avoid illness and further complications.

As with anything, there is a correct time and place for everything. Do not promote your black son to have girlfriends and date early in life. Eight, nine, ten year olds should not be thinking about girlfriends and dating – this promotes other behaviors and can lead to unwanted pregnancies. The same approach applies to fatherhood– tell your son at what age it is appropriate to think about fatherhood: after securing an education, job skill and traveling. I

gave my son an age bracket when he can start thinking about marrying and having a family – so far it is working. As a young man, your black son will think about sex – a lot – but it is up to <u>you</u> to keep positively reinforcing education, traveling – other life experiences to obtain before fatherhood.

Today's society places an extreme emphasis on sex. The young black man feels pressured to procreate because society tells him he is not going to live past a certain age. Direct your son down a different path – away from the hype – a leader never rushes into anything – including parenting. Being a king also means providing for one's kingdom.

Sexual Preference and the Black Son

Let me start by saying – my son is not a homosexual. From a very young age my son has been attracted to the opposite sex. I am saying this because you the black mother are aware of your black's son's behaviors from a very young age. Now is not the time to be in denial, to use your religion as a shield of judgment. God is the only one to judge and although we are made in His image – we are NOT GOD!!! DO NOT JUDGE YOUR BLACK SON.

I have counseled many parents who have faced this situation. It is important to get as much factual information as possible from medical professionals. First of all, this is not about you. This is your black son – love him unconditionally. Secondly, please keep the following in mind:

Fear and ignorance kills – please don't let your black son become a victim.

Homosexuals are NOT pedophiles! Some of my dearest friends are homosexuals/lesbians and my son and I love them completely. My son and I have been very fortunate to receive the love, support and respect from our friends, who just happen to be homosexuals and lesbians. Just because my son and I have friends who happen to be homosexuals/lesbians, does not mean they are trying to influence us in any way.

What goes on behind closed doors is their business – period.

You must talk with your black son openly and have complete trust. People are killed for expressing their sexual preference openly as the result of homophobia. Speculation, alienation and hostility can kill your black son. Teach your black son about taking the proper precautions in sexual activity, where he socializes and with whom.

Many parents have informed me that they noticed their son's attraction to the same gender/sex from an early age. Make sure your black son has not been abused sexually. Get the help of your son's pediatrician, go on line and obtain information that is valid and do not ever believe that your black son can be sent to a camp and brainwashed into being a heterosexual.

Almost any local college/university will have a LGBT Alliance Organization (Lesbian, Gay, Bisexual, Transgendered) that can offer you support groups as well as tons of resources. http://www.glaad.org/

Many parents I have helped faced fear of their son being harmed and the fear of backlash from the community they live in. Your black son is vulnerable here as he is trying to find his niche as a black young man who is also homosexual. This acceptance can cause depression, drug/alcohol use and risky behaviors to gain acceptance. Peer pressure is extreme and your son needs to me armed and ready to face the world. Your black son needs your love and support of him. Your acceptance and understanding supports your black son to go on and have a good life; aspiring to his dreams. Continue to hug him, kiss him and be active in his life; please do not judge your black son or disown him.

Remember, ignorance & fear kills – protect your black son from the violence of homophobia. If your black son is gay, get help and keep your black son safe.

Remember –denial can kill.

Keeping Your Sexuality Separate from Your Son's Sexuality.

Keep your sexual business to yourself – that's why I advised you earlier in this book to take your sex business outside of the home you share with your son. Never let your son into your relationship drama. Respect your son and yourself – you don't have to walk around your house buck naked – there will be a time when your son will see you naked and that is fine.

There may be time or two when your son may have to see you in the most compromising situation: home sick with the flu, sitting on the toilet with the wastepaper basket in your lap so you can puke and shit at the same time. You may get something even more serious – like a fall down the flight of stairs. Your so has to be taught at an early age to remain calm and level headed – seeing you ill, fallen and injured is bad enough – don't let this be the first time your son sees you naked!

Your son does not need to be involved in any of your relationship issues. Watch what you say and when you say it. Remember—an altercation, fight or argument with your partner in front of your son involves him and could quickly escalate into violence and even death. If the above describes your own life; if you are a lesbian or bisexual, use discretion in how much information and at what age to discuss this with your black son. Trust is paramount.

Be a Pal Sometimes - ALWAYS Be a Mom!!!

I always tell my son: "I am your mom, not your friend!" This is a serious boundary that was discovered back in the relationship chapter. My son and I are not roommates either. Sure we hang out, travel and have a blast, but when the day is done – I am still mom. This level of respect cannot be moved as I do not treat my son like a friend by doing inappropriate things with or in front of my son and vice-versa. I don't party with my son. Yes, my son has tried to fix me up with single men – he wants me to date and that is normal. My son also knows his place and I know mine. We are both happy in our places and we have grown tremendously in them as well.

Too many times we have read or heard in the news of parents doing inappropriate things with their kids. Don't be one of these parents. You son needs boundaries and structure – give it to him – it's his right! Too many times I witness mothers having inappropriate conversations in the presence of their son's. "He's just a baby, he can't understand." Think again. Children are sponges, soaking up everything around them and if they do not utilize that information, now – they will later. Society has evolved to the point where there is little or no censorship when it comes to children. The result of this continued irresponsible action is children doing inappropriate behaviors and parents being totally unaccountable. Censorship is a necessary part of parenting. Let your black son be a child for as long as possible.

Have Your Black Son's Back.

Yes! You can kick ass and really defend your son – you are supposed to! Advocate for your son and let the community know that this black child is yours and you will not tolerate **anyone** messing with him! Trust your son and let your black son earn your trust. Please keep in mind that you will have to earn your black son's trust as well. Security and protection are two components of parenting that your black son needs. These two components help build self-esteem, confidence, validity, and as I stated above, trust.

Historically, as a result of slavery our children do not feel safe, do not trust as easily. A child that trusts and truly loves his mother will also try to protect her as well. Stand up for your black son and cheer for him, vouch for him and give him a voice. Sometimes having your son's back becomes national news: Genarlow Wilson was sentenced for ten years for having consensual oral sex with a 15 year old when he was 17 years old at a New Year's Eve party in 2003. A party where drugs, alcohol and teens were all present; were these teens replicating a hip-hop video? A partygoer videotaped Wilson and the female. The tape became evidence against Wilson and a jury found him guilty. Jaunnessa Bennett, Genarlow's mother is a black single parent of two children.

After her son was prosecuted, convicted and sentenced to prison, Jaunnessa had a good hard cry and went into battle mode. Those survival skills discussed earlier kick up and kicked out. They would call her the crazy lady but Jaunnessa sacrificed sleep and worked. She retained white female lawyer and campaigned to the media about her son's plight which up until that time went unrecognized by the media.

Jaunnessa was a quiet, hardworking single black mother. When she saw her son being taken by the system, Jaunessa became a tsunami in the predominately white southern community of Georgia. Jaunnessa went up against a huge, traditionally white, powerful entity called the white south. Georgia State Senator Vincent Fort, a supporter of the Wilson case states: "I have no doubt that

Genarlow would still be in jail if it weren't for his mother." (Thomas, August 2008). Jaunnessa, the dignified and humble queen that she is hopes: "My story inspires others out there fighting for their children caught in the system." (Thomas, August 2008)*. Of course, Genarlow best describes his situation: "She (my mother) was there for me when no one else was."

My Grandmother used to say: "A mother's love saves. When the world says kill him, a mother will be the only voice heard asking to save her child." Have your black son's back. You may save his life.

*Thomas, Chandra. R, "Dear Mama: The Nation & the World Protested Genarlow Wilson's Controversial Prison Sentence. But it was his mother who pulled him through the fight of his life." Ebony Magazine. August 2008. Pgs. 115-117.

The Death Talk.

Death is serious – it's permanent. Death comes in many forms to many people. A black child has to understand this early because blacks have the highest and earliest death rate of any race. Your black son has to understand the grieving process and the many forms of death. Adolescents feel invincible and disassociate with death. Death reminds us of our mortality. Risky behaviors in cars, with sex, guns or drugs can result in death. Your black son is exposed to this everyday he walks out of your sanctuary and goes off into the world. He could be killed walking to school, at a party, at the mall, anywhere. He could have a disagreement with someone, he could be defending someone or just wearing the wrong color that day – I have witnessed many scenarios.

My suggestion to you is to talk with your son about the following that as an adolescent/teen can place him in death's path before his time:

* Do not let friends drive drunk – do not get in a car with a drunk driver.

* Do not experiment with drugs.

* Do not go to parties where gangs are.

* Do not fight over a girl.

* Do not defend a girl unless you know exactly what went down.

* If you do get into a fight with someone and they tell you: "I'll be back!" get the hell up outta there!

* Wear a condom when having sex.

* Just say "No thanks" it could save your life. * Be mindful of walking up to a car that pulls over to you.

* If a friend asks you to hold a package for them – don't.

Talking about the above topics is important in understanding your son's daily life and what he is exposed to when he is out of your home. Don't assume anything.

Chapter Eight

On the Brink of Being a King

Networking Your Black Son.

You have groomed your son, this future king – now you need to connect him to the right people – as the saying goes: "It's not always what you know but whom you know." From a very young age my son has been out in our community right along with me and my work as a Community Activist and Social Worker. Networking the youth is done in other races all the time. I witnessed the importance of networking when my son was fundraising for his trip to Australia. Jordan went out into the community, attended community meetings and rubbed elbows with law enforcement, politicians and community leaders.

This exposure along with my son's demeanor (speech, attitude and dress) resulted in my son obtaining donations that helped sponsor his trip. Jordan now has affiliates in many areas of our community that has resulted in his recognition and respect in our community. He was able to network on the golf course, at local community meetings and of course through his school activities. Networking your son opens up his views and destroys stigmas. Once the bridge of networking has been built – your son will walk over this bridge that he created time and time again.

Your networking black son must adapt an appearance that is non-threatening (Remember what we discussed earlier about Michelle Obama and other prominent black women? Well guess what? Black men have the same thing occurring). The approach is for your black son is to adopt an attitude of 'cultural archaeology', that is your son must examine what he can about the white world and take this knowledge and use it to his advantage. No one is saying your son has to sell out – but if your son wants to get along, succeed and forge a life for himself this is my suggestion for him.

Society still believes blacks to be inferior, out of control and unproductive. Here is another example: A young black male teen has to appear at his law guardian's office. The young black man would later reveal to his mother that: "The attorney did a double take when I walked through the door... He (Attorney) kept remarking how articulate and well dressed I was... he even remarked on the golf magazine I had in my hand. I could feel that this man really had other expectations on what I would present when I came to his office...He was so impressed with what I was doing in school that he invited me to shadow him for a day at work."

The mother replied: "That is great, but the funny thing is in court, your law guardian cannot remember my name, but he remembers your father's name very well. Son, if you want to get a first hand view of an attorney's work day in court – then accept his invitation gladly, if not then whenever you see him again greet him respectfully , you never know when you will have need of his services or connections."

The single black mother understands the viability of having connections and she also understands that the attorney expected to see her son as the media has programmed America and the world: cornrows, baggy jeans hanging off his ass with his underwear showing, a big chain around his neck and some gold teeth or maybe a few tattoos across his forehead. What this white man did witness is an articulate, well-groomed black male teen **that can hold his own and not be intimidated by**

authority. Networking your black son is a self esteem builder as well as an incentive for grooming and speaking well. Being familiar and a part of one's community is an asset that grows into community service and leadership.

Travel and the Black Son.

Any opportunity given to your black son to travel – TAKE IT!!! Remember – Gandhi and Jesus both traveled in their lifetime as well as Malcolm X. Traveling broadens your black son's awareness as well as allows him to represent his race/gender. Traveling breaks down barriers. Traveling allows your son to be resourceful upon him-self and what he remembered to pack for his trip! You black son's exposure to traveling will discipline him to a behavior that will make him be aware of time, be accountable of where he has to be and how he communicates with people.

Traveling to other countries and cultures broadens your black son's exposure and he will be more tolerant of others not like himself as well as possess a comfort to represent himself. He may also try something new that he has never had an opportunity to do in the past at home for whatever reason. People to People is an excellent resource for your son to travel and earn school credits. It will require fundraising but it is well worth the effort.

Get your black son a passport! This vital identification is literally your son's passport to the world. Remember—President Obama is a well traveled man from childhood. Notice Obama's demeanor with people—all people. Having that early exposure supports his comfort with diversity. If and when your black son is given the opportunity to travel – TAKE IT!!! Host fund raisers, borrow travel gear from friends, and don't allow a few challenges to deter you and your black son from having this experience. Yes, I included you – when your son comes home, whom do you think he is going to tell EVERY detail of his trip to? YOU!

Step out, take a chance with your black son for your black son and watch him grow. **A goal such as this takes your son out of the neighborhood and this alone is a wonderful incentive. Many young black men never leave the hood, they ascribe to staying on familiar ground even if it means missing opportunities and befriending negative people.**

College, Vocational School or Armed Service.

Your black son needs to hear about college continually from you very early on in his life. I know of young people right here in my community who have never step foot inside a college or university—the amazing thing is I happen to live in a five college town! If your black son lives in a small city or town, encourage him to get the hell up outta there! There is more to life and this world for your black son to experience and getting out of your hometown is key to broadening his views. Early immersion into higher education has the same rewards as early reading and math—the black son is strong, confident and has goals of enhancing what he has been exposed to. **It is not a matter of if but when!**

College is an opportunity at higher learning, an exposure to different people, places and concepts. Upward Bound is a great program that promotes higher education to high school students. I cannot guarantee you that your black son will not encounter situations and professors as described by Dr. Stevens in the Education Chapter—it is vital to teach and guide your black son to work around racism and the people who practice it. How well your black son navigates this disgusting practice will determine his level of success—after all that is their issue, not your black son's. There will definitely be times when your black son must face racism—what you teach in your sanctuary, your home will guide him and he will handle himself accordingly, if necessary, you may have to step in and advocate so be ready.

Applying for scholarships and grants to afford college is necessary—don't let your own experiences with education affect your black son's chances. Now is the time to tap into all the networking and your son's mentor for guidance and advice. DO NOT RELY UPON YOUR BLACK SON'S SCHOOL/GUIDANCE OFFICE TO HELP. As discussed in the education chapter, many guidance offices deter blacks from higher education.

Do inquire about SAT/ACT vouchers so your son may take the exam for free. Also, keep a copy of your son's graduation requirements posted on the refrigerator at home and keep track of what classes your son is taking— too many black males do not graduate with a diploma because they are lacking the necessary classes required in your state to obtain a diploma. That's why it is VITAL that you remain actively participating in your black son's education. The education system in America is flawed and it is NOT friendly towards black males but rather a systematic push for your black son to end up in an orange suit rather than a Brooks Brothers suit. **Remember—there is a profit being made by someone for every black man sitting in prison today.**

There are free SAT/ACT prep classes and of courses at the local library and on line information with practice questions and lots of guidance—found at: http://www.collegeboard.com/ your son should be getting ready and also taking the PSAT in 10th grade. I have witnessed firsthand parents of other ethnicities preparing their children as early as 8th grade to college—there is a high level of completion of students in this area and sadly the black male is sparse in attendance. The many college tours and prep classes my son and I visited showed little if any black male participation—if there were black males present, pretty soon we saw the same ones at all the other places we visited. How daunting this must be for a black young man to be surrounded by so many UNLIKE him! It is up to YOU to cheer your black son on and 12th grade will be the hardest test of just how much does your black son and his family wants him to further his education. Don't give up, don't let go and don't stop being diligent on what your son is doing now because he is close to 18, or there already. Now is the time to REALLY keep tabs on him. The devil is busy, especially when one is on the threshold of success! Your son my want to party and whoop it up in 12th grade = BIG MISTAKE!!

Now is the time to push the networking and stay at home away from parties and trouble. Now I the time to be working on applying for scholarships, writing essays and getting those letters of recommendation. **Now the real work begins.**

If your son wants to attend vocational school— great—let him intern and shadow professionals in the field he is interested in—this is where the networking comes in! Vocational school is great for carpentry, plumbing, electrical and more. Your son may have a talent in these areas and this is such a self esteem boost – let him develop these hands on skills and build his future with them. Many of these skills are in high demand and pay very well.

The Armed Services is also a wonderful opportunity, just make sure your son is not being forced by a recruiter making grand promises that will not be kept. Ask your black son to please keep you in the communication loop with the armed services – and to put you down as a person of contact and authority to know his affairs.

ALL OF THE ABOVE REQUIRES YOU TO TALK AND LISTEN TO YOUR BLACK SON.

***The one concept that is bound to occur and is a negative of peer pressure: Your black son's friends may act differently towards him as they witness him getting closer to his goals of college, vocational school or the armed services. As your black son wins scholarships, stays home away from tempting parties and such and is getting closer to changing his life, many of his peers may demonstrate resentment and even ostracize him. Talk with your son about this phenomenon and encourage him to hold fast to his own goals that he has worked all his life for.**

Technology, Guns & Violence.

There is so much in the news about boys, violence and anger—I had to incorporate a section in my book about this.

Violence concerning guns is growing in younger, white males; often who were trained how to shoot by their fathers in a father-son bonding exercise called hunting. Many of these young white boys had a gun made especially for them. There are guns in the home and hunting is an accepted part of white culture. Observe how society will prosecute these young white boys who are shooting and killing their families.

Black young boys get guns from the street as part of gang activity as the result of low socioeconomics and no one at home to provide the self esteem building; this deficit results in the young black son going out to the streets to obtain validation and self worth in the worst way—gang participation. Prosecution is often harsh in the judicial system for the black son.

So, here we have a white son who learns how to shoot from dad and then we have the black son who learns how to shoot as part of gang related violence— which do you think society will absolve?

Today's young men are different than the young men their father's were due to the influence of technology. There are many benefits to technology but at the same time there are deficits as well. Technology demands faster, better intense actions from remote or often distant locations. The internet has placed me anywhere in the world that I type into. I can obtain all kinds of data, picture and sounds—virtual reality but there is a difference. I am not actually present; there's a disconnect. I am not using my brain to the fullest: my five senses are not all engaged and my ability to use judgment/assessment is impaired or hindered because of physically where I am NOT.

Video games can be fun and entertaining. Unfortunately, many games are focused on high violence: murder, rape, drugs, etc. Graphics are so real the brain thinks it is actually in the moment. Many games come with rating systems so that society knows which games are for children and which games are for adults. More adult games are mainstreamed around children than we think. For example: Disney Quest, a multi floored indoor arcade has games from air hockey to foot controlled virtual games—all of these games are together, the shooting games are with the fighting that is with the space aliens, etc. Many parents, in order to keep the peace in their home and to also keep up with the Joneses buy their children games that are NOT age appropriate—some kids get these games without their parents even being aware they own them. Here is the problem:

Children are children, their minds are NOT fully developed neither is their sense of reality, judgment or logic. Take a high tech, virtual reality video game that fakes the brain because it is so real and now you have a child who is desensitized between reality and virtual reality. The child is desensitized to violence, sex, drugs, and profanity. What may shock you does not faze a child who has been exposed to these games in the least.

If you have any doubts, talk with a teacher and ask how children discuss sex in school. This has increased ten-fold with teachers reporting children as young as five having intercourse in the classroom closet. Notes passed between boys & girls as young as seven describing blow jobs, anal sex and desires of pregnancy. School fights, children run to watch with animated faces and act like they are watching a circus, not violence that can seriously hurt or even kill. Children are dressing in very suggestive clothing with no concern or concept as to what kind of attention the attire will attract.

Radio lyrics have changed, now on the radio 'ass' 'bitch' hoe' as well as very graphic in detail descriptions about sex are blaring over the air waves—when I was growing up—you never heard this type of language on the radio. I think Maude was the first person to use the word 'bitch' on television.

Because of technology parents have taken a laid back approach to parenting. Because of technology our children are being born today more alert and newborns are practically talking before going home. The stimulation of technology has desensitized both parents and children alike.

Keep it real with your black son. Do not allow the behaviors described above in your home, your sanctuary and please monitor your black son's video gaming activities. It is best to get your son out of his room and engaged in swimming, karate, playing music, other sports and engaging with people. This activity will also diminish weight gain which is so prevalent in today's children who are grossly obese.

Your black son has to understand the difference between dating violence and domestic violence and how BOTH are simply not tolerated. VIOLENCE AGAINST ANY HUMAN BEING IS WRONG. Unfortunately, both domestic and dating violence has the male as the aggressor/perpetrator this goes back in history: white women were chattel—black women were slaves. Men, husbands were allowed to beat their wives with a stick no bigger than their thumb = The Rule of Thumb.

Now of course, the media picks and chooses what to focus upon and you the single black mom must always be aware of this. Raising a male child has opened my eyes to the male view of violence in relationships and I am against having violence be gender focused—dating violence and domestic violence is wrong period. To place such emphasis on gender is simply not equitable to human beings as a whole. I have seen countless acts of violence done to men by their wives, girlfriends or baby mamas. There was a song out last year that was played on the radio constantly: the lyrics began with "I broke the windows out your car…" The girl was singing about what she did to her ex because he was dating someone else. The male ego won't let these cases become public in high profile but they do exist. I have seen young girls get black sons killed over a lie—a spoken word. I would like to see no gender separation between dating/domestic violence but treated equally with the same concern and prosecution.

The cell phone—the love/ hate relationship. I cannot remember my life without it. If I leave it at home, I go back and I get it. The cell phone makes me accessible 24/7—even on the toilet. The cell phone is a young person's best friend. When you don't pay the bill and the service is turned off—watch your black son lose weight and become a different person!

For you the black single mom—the cell phone is a viable connection between you and your son. Your black son needs to understand that this cell phone is also a weapon that could kill him or put him in prison. A cell phone logs calls, messages and photos. You would be surprised how many girls send your black son naked pictures of themselves to his phone. You may also have received a few sexy pictures from the guy you are talking to. STOP—these photos can become admissible evidence is child custody cases and if the girl who sent your black

son the naked pictures of herself happens to be a minor—
then that is pornography and your son could be charged.

Your son goes to a party and takes pictures of
people drinking, having sex, smoking dope—all could
become evidence in court and your black son can end up
in prison. Ask Genarlow Wilson—his example I used in
"Having your black son's back" Mr. Wilson's cell phone
implicated him having oral sex from a consenting girl at a
party who was under age = prison sentence. Ask Michael
Phelps—he was photographed by a cell phone while
smoking from a bong.

Text messaging about drugs, sex, criminal activity
all can be traced on a cell phone—throw always
(disposable phones) are almost traceable as well. Driving
while texting or on the cell phone can also cause car
accidents, even death. The cell phone is quickly becoming
the new gun for the young black son as far as evidence and
jail time. Talk to your son about this and please—**have a
cell phone curfew during school months**.

Chapter Nine

Contracts

These Contracts Are For You & Your Black Son. Put Your Name and Your Son's Name Where Appropriate and Let These Oaths (Vows) Strengthen You Towards Truth, Success and Love!

Motherhood

I _____ take this sacred vow that this baby that I carry in My womb will remain drug free, violence free and be born healthy; welcomed In love and be treated as the miracle God has intended. I _____ understand this distinction of being a mother will take all that I am, it will change me but I will not give up on my baby or myself. I shall continue to develop myself to be the best person I can be for my son. No addiction, no relationship shall come between me and my son. My signature on my son's birth certificate designates me as being the responsible And accountable constant parent in my son's life in all aspects. I_____ understand that my child is innocent, defenseless and totally reliant upon my guidance, judgment, participation, attitude and behavior. My son needs affection, protection, nutrition and education. My baby has the potential to be the best individual in the world and my son is valuable and precious as well as a gift from God. My baby, my son shall be treated with Respect, Reverence and Responsibility.

_____Your Signature/Date

_____Witnessed By/Date

Parenting

I _____ understand that I am my son's parent, not his friend. My parenting will involve responsibility and accountability with participation. There will be censorship and mature understanding that my son is a child and is not an adult and will not be exposed to nor treated as such. I _____ understand that I am a parent for LIFE and that my needs are NOT paramount. I _____ shall conduct myself as a mature, reliable, responsible & accountable individual who is fully aware that my son needs me as an active, positive presence in his life. I _____ understand that neglect indifference, irresponsibility and non-commitment are not a part of my being a parent and will only result in failure & a breakdown of boundaries.
CONTINUED ON NEXT PAGE...

I _____ will make every effort with every essence of my being to support my son in every area of his life. I _____ will listen, act and support my son to the best of my ability, putting my own issues aside. I _____ as a parent will be available for My son, for my son and because my son is MINE!!! No one can replace the care I give him, no one knows him like I do. God put us together and only God can separate us.

_____

Your Signature/Date

_____

_Witnessed By/Date

Black Young Son

I _____, son

of_____

promise not to lie to my mother. I promise to talk to my Mother and share my day **every** day with her. I _____, son of _____ Will NOT do drugs, be around guns or practice unprotected sexual activity. I _____ am a black son of

_____

and I will maintain pride, self control and hard work that reflect my appreciation, respect and responsibility to my mother, myself, my ancestors, my country and God.

_____

Son Signature/Date

_____

Mother's Signature/Date

Education Oath

I _____ will attend school every day. I will do my school work and homework. I will communicate with my Mother at all times as to what is going on in school. I _____ will support my son in his Education at all grade levels.

We_____

and_____

understand that Education saves lives and is very important to the black man, woman and child.

I_____ have the potential to become anything positive in this world. I have the power to say NO to ignorance and stigmas. We have the power to say NO to poor choices._____ Mother Sign/Date

_____Son Sign/Date

Home Contract

I_____

promise to keep my home a sanctuary; a place of peace, rest and safety for myself and my son_____.
There are no drugs, violence, profanity or sexual misconduct in this sacred space. I will tend to this home with cleanliness, organization and harmony. In this home my black son and I have respect, trust, confidence and safety. In our home God lives with us always.

_____Your Signature/Date.

The Black Man's Future

I_____ put God first in my life.

I_____ will remain focused upon my goals and feed my dreams with positive actions and education so that I will be successful.

I_____

understand that I must work hard and sacrifice to have a future. I must say NO to drugs, alcohol, unprotected sex and violence. I

_____

understand that I am the product of generations of Continued on Next Page.

ancestors who died so that I may live. I am part of a heritage of strength and courage. I _____ am loved and I am valued, therefore I value myself. I will not be a father until I am _____years old.

I will find a woman with similar goals and positive action and she will be my wife. We will build a family together.

I_____ am able to be a good father and husband. I will provide for and protect my family with my name and my intelligence and my presence. I understand the responsibilities of being a King.

_____

Black Son Sign/Date

Chapter Ten
Developmental Assets & Your Future King (Toddler-High School)

Lots of factors influence how our kids grow up and the choices they make, including whether they use alcohol. When life gets complicated, it can be easy to forget the basics—the foundation that helps kids make positive choices in many areas of life. Search Institute's widely used framework of Developmental Assets offers a practical, positive strategy for making a difference.

What are Developmental Assets?
Grounded in scientific research, Developmental Assets are 40 essential building blocks of healthy development. Think of assets as the "good stuff" that young people need in their lives to help them grow up healthy, caring, and responsible. As a parent, you play a vital role in building these assets—both in how you relate to your child and how you connect your child with other caring people and places in your family and community.

Why do Developmental Assets matter? Research shows that the more Developmental Assets young people experience, the less likely they are to engage in a wide range of high-risk behaviors including underage drinking, violence, illicit drug use, sexual activity, gambling, eating disorders and school truancy. Just as important, the more assets they experience, the more likely they are to engage in positive or thriving behaviors, such as succeeding in school, helping others, maintaining good health and overcoming adversity. Taking a positive, asset-building approach to parenting isn't glamorous or a "miracle cure." It doesn't take away all the irritations and frustrations that are inevitable in parenting. And it doesn't guarantee that nothing will go wrong. But building assets does increase the odds that your child will grow up well. It affirms the many ways you are already making a difference. It encourages you when you're wondering if anything is getting through. And it reminds you that the little stuff does, in the end, add up to make a big difference.

The Following Pages are the 40 Developmental Assets: Toddler, Middle & High School.

Please read the developmental assets and you will see the relationship of these assets supporting the parenting actions described in this book.

40 Developmental Assets for Early Childhood (ages 3-5)
EXTERNAL ASSETS

SUPPORT

Family Support | Parents and/or primary caregivers provide the child with high levels of consistent and predictable love, physical care, and positive attention in ways that are responsive to the child's individuality.

Positive Family Communication | Parents and/or primary caregivers express themselves positively and respectfully, engaging young children in conversations that invite their input.

Other Adult Relationships | With the family's support, the child experiences consistent, caring relationships with adults outside the family.

Caring Neighborhood | The child's network of relationships includes neighbors who provide emotional support and a sense of belonging.

Caring Climate in Child Care and Educational Settings | Caregivers and teachers create environments that are nurturing, accepting, encouraging, and secure.

Parent Involvement in Child Care and Education | Parents, caregivers, and teachers together create a consistent and supportive approach to fostering the child's successful growth.

EMPOWERMENT

Community Cherishes and Values Young Children | Children are welcomed and included throughout community life.

Children Seen as Resources | The community demonstrates that children are valuable resources by investing in a child-rearing system of family support and high-quality activities and resources to meet children's physical, social, and emotional needs.

Service to Others | The child has opportunities to perform simple but meaningful and caring actions for others.

Safety | Parents, caregivers, teachers, neighbors, and the community take action to ensure children's health and safety.

BOUNDARIES & EXPECTATIONS

Family Boundaries | The family provides consistent supervision for the child and maintains reasonable guidelines for behavior that the child can understand and achieve.

Boundaries in Child Care and Educational Settings | Caregivers and educators use positive approaches to discipline and natural consequences to encourage self-regulation and acceptable behaviors.

Neighborhood Boundaries | Neighbors encourage the child in positive, acceptable behavior, as well as intervene in negative behavior, in a supportive, nonthreatening way.

Adult Role Models | Parents and other adults model self-control, social skills, engagement in learning, and healthy lifestyles.

Positive Peer Relationships | Parents and caregivers seek to provide opportunities for the child to interact positively with other children.

Positive Expectations | Parent(s), caregivers, and teachers encourage and support the child in behaving appropriately, undertaking challenging tasks, and performing activities to the best of her or his abilities.

CONSTRUCTIVE USE OF TIME

Play and Creative Activities | The child has daily opportunities to play in ways that allow self-expression, physical activity, and interaction with others.

Out-of-Home and Community Programs | The child experiences well-designed programs led by competent, caring adults in well-maintained settings.

Religious Community | The child participates in age-appropriate religious activities and caring relationships that nurture her or his spiritual development.

Time at Home | The child spends most of her or his time at home participating in family activities and playing constructively, with parents guiding TV and electronic game use.

INTERNAL ASSETS

COMMITMENT TO LEARNING

Motivation to Mastery | The child responds to new experiences with curiosity and energy, resulting in the pleasure of mastering new learning and skills.

Engagement in Learning Experiences | The child fullyparticipates in a variety of activities that offer opportunities for learning.

Home-program Connection | The child experiences security, consistency, and connections between home and out-of-home care programs and learning activities.

Bonding to Programs | The child forms meaningful connections with out-of-home care and educational programs.

Early Literacy | The child enjoys a variety of pre-reading activities, including adults reading to him or her daily, looking at and handling books, playing with a variety of media, and showing interest in pictures, letters, and numbers.

POSITIVE VALUES

Caring | The child begins to show empathy, understanding, and awareness of others' feelings.
Equality and Social Justice | The child begins to show concern for people who are excluded from play and other activities or are not treated fairly because they are different.

Integrity | The child begins to express her or his views appropriately and to stand up for a growing sense of what is fair and right.

Honesty | The child begins to understand the difference between truth and lies, and is truthful to the extent of her or his understanding.

Responsibility | The child begins to follow through on simple tasks to take care of her- or himself and to help others.

Self-regulation | The child can increasingly identify, regulate, and control her or his behaviors in healthy ways and use adult support constructively in particularly stressful situations.

SOCIAL COMPETENCIES

Planning and Decision Making | The child begins to plan forthe immediate future, choosing from among several options and trying to solve problems.

Interpersonal Skills | The child cooperates, shares, plays harmoniously, and comforts others in distress.

Cultural Awareness and Sensitivity | The child begins to learn about her or his own cultural identity and to show acceptance of people who are racially, physically, culturally, or ethnically different from him or her.

Resistance Skills | The child begins to sense danger accurately, to seek help from trusted adults, and to resist pressure from peers to participate in unacceptable or risky behavior.

Peaceful Conflict Resolution | The child begins to compromise and resolve conflicts without using physical aggression or hurtful language.

POSITIVE IDENTITY

Personal Power | The child can make choices that give a sense of having some influence over things that happen in her or his life.

Self-Esteem | The child likes her- or himself and has a growing sense of being valued by others.

Sense of Purpose | The child anticipates new opportunities, experiences, and milestones in growing up.

Positive View of Personal Future | The child finds the world interesting and enjoyable, and feels that he or she has a positive place in it.

This list is an educational tool. It is not intended to be nor is it appropriate as a scientific measure of the developmental assets of individuals.

40 Developmental Assets for Middle Childhood (ages 8–12)

EXTERNAL ASSETS

SUPPORT

Family Support | Family life provides high levels of love and support.

Positive Family Communication | Parent(s) and child communicate positively. Child feels comfortable seeking advice and counsel from parent(s).

Other Adult Relationships | Child receives support from adults other than her or his parent(s).

Caring Neighborhood | Child person experiences caring neighbors.

Caring School Climate | Relationships with teachers and peers provide a caring, encouraging environment.

Parent Involvement in Schooling | Parent(s) are actively involved in helping the child succeed in school.

EMPOWERMENT

Community Values Youth | Child feels valued and appreciated by adults in the community.

Children as Resources | Child is included in decisions at home and in the community.

Service to Others | Child has opportunities to help others in the community. **Safety** | Child feels safe at home, school, and in the neighborhood.

BOUNDARIES AND EXPECTATIONS

Family Boundaries | Family has clear rules and consequences and monitors the child 's whereabouts.

School Boundaries | School provides clear rules and consequences.

Neighborhood Boundaries | Neighbors take responsibility for monitoring the child's behavior.

Adult Role Models | Parent(s) and other adults in the child's family, as well as nonfamily adults, model positive, responsible behavior.

Positive Peer Influence | Child's closest friends model positive, responsible behavior.
High Expectations | Parent(s) and teachers expect the child to do her or his best at school and in other activities.

CONSTRUCTIVE USE OF TIME
Creative Activities | Child participates in music, art, drama, or creative writing two or more times per week.
Child Programs |Child participates two or more times per week in co curricular school activities or structured community programs for children.
Religious Community | Child attends religious programs or services one or more times per week.

Time at Home | Child spends some time most days both in high-quality interaction with parents and doing things at home other than watching TV or playing video games.

INTERNAL ASSETS

COMMITMENT TO LEARNING

Achievement Motivation | Child is motivated and strives to do well in school.

Learning Engagement | Child is responsive, attentive, and actively engaged in learning at school and enjoys participating in learning activities outside of school.
Homework | Child usually hands in homework on time.
Bonding to School | Child cares about teachers and other adults at school.

Reading for Pleasure | Child enjoys and engages in reading for fun most days of the week.

POSITIVE VALUES

Caring | Parent(s) tell the child it is important to help other people.

Equality and Social Justice | Parent(s) tell the child it is important to speak up for equal rights for all people.

Integrity | Parent(s) tell the child it is important to stand up for one's beliefs.

Honesty | Parent(s) tell the child it is important to tell the truth.

Responsibility | Parent(s) tell the child it is important to accept personal responsibility for behavior.

Healthy Lifestyle | Parent(s) tell the child it is important to have good health habits and an understanding of healthy sexuality.

SOCIAL COMPETENCIES

Planning and Decision Making | Child thinks about decisions and is usually happy with results of her or his decisions.
Interpersonal Competence | Child cares about and is affected by other people's feelings, enjoys making friends, and, when frustrated or angry, tries to calm her- or himself.
Interpersonal Competence | Young person has empathy, sensitivity, and friendship skills.

Cultural Competence | Child knows and is comfortable with people of different racial, ethnic, and cultural backgrounds and with her or his own cultural identity.

Resistance Skills | Child can stay away from people who are likely to get her or him in trouble and is able to say no to doing wrong or dangerous things.

Peaceful Conflict Resolution | Child seeks to resolve conflict nonviolently.

POSITIVE IDENTITY

Personal Power | Child feels he or she has some influence over things that happen in her or his life.

Self-Esteem | Child likes and is proud to be the person that he or she is.

Sense of Purpose | Child sometimes thinks about what life means and whether there is a purpose for her or his life.
Positive View of Personal Future | Child is optimistic about her or his personal future.

40 Developmental Assets for adolescents (ages 12-18)

EXTERNAL ASSETS
SUPPORT

Family Support | Family life provides high levels of love and support.

 Positive Family Communication | Parent(s) and child communicate positively. Child feels comfortable seeking advice and counsel from parent(s).

Other Adult Relationships | Child receives support from adults other than her or his parent(s).

Caring Neighborhood | Child person experiences caring neighbors.

Caring School Climate | Relationships with teachers and peers provide a caring, encouraging environment.

Parent Involvement in Schooling | Parent(s) are actively involved in helping the child succeed in school.

EMPOWERMENT

Community Values Youth | Child feels valued and appreciated by adults in the community.

Children as Resources | Child is included in decisions at home and in the community.

Service to Others | Child has opportunities to help others in the community.

Safety | Child feels safe at home, school, and in the neighborhood. BOUNDARIES AND EXPECTATIONS

Family Boundaries | Family has clear rules and consequences and monitors the child's whereabouts.

School Boundaries | School provides clear rules and consequences.

Neighborhood Boundaries | Neighbors take responsibility for monitoring the child's behavior.

Adult Role Models | Parent(s) and other adults in the child's family, as well as nonfamily adults, model positive, responsible behavior.

Positive Peer Influence | Child's closest friends model positive, responsible behavior.

High Expectations | Parent(s) and teachers expect the child to do her or his best at school and in other activities

CONSTRUCTIVE USE OF TIME

Creative Activities | Child participates in music, art, drama, or creative writing two or more times per week. **Child Programs** | Child participates two or more times per week in co curricular school activities or structured community programs for children.

Religious Community | Child attends religious programs or services one or more times per week.

Time at Home | Child spends some time most days both in high-quality interaction with parents and doing things at home other than watching TV or playing video games.

INTERNAL ASSETS

COMMITMENT TO LEARNING

Achievement Motivation | Young person is motivated to do well in school.

School Engagement | Young person is actively engaged in learning.

Homework | Young person reports doing at least one hour of homework every school day.

Bonding to School | Young person cares about her or his school.

Reading for Pleasure | Young person reads for pleasure three or more hours per week.

POSITIVE VALUES

Caring | Young Person places high value on helping other people.

Equality and Social Justice | Young person places high value on promoting equality and reducing hunger and poverty.

Integrity | Young person acts on convictions and stands up for her or his beliefs.

Honesty | Young person "tells the truth even when it is not easy."

Responsibility | Young person accepts and takes personal responsibility.

Restraint | Young person believes it is important not to be sexually active or to use alcohol or other drugs.

SOCIAL COMPETENCIES

Planning and Decision Making | Young person knows how to plan ahead and make choices.

Interpersonal Competence | Young person has empathy, sensitivity, and friendship skills.

Cultural Competence | Young person has knowledge of and comfort with people of different cultural/racial/ethnic backgrounds.

Resistance Skills | Young person can resist negative peer pressure and dangerous situations.

Peaceful Conflict Resolution | Young person seeks to resolve conflict nonviolently.

POSITIVE IDENTITY

Personal Power | Young person feels he or she has control over "things that happen to me."

Self-Esteem | Young person reports having a high self-esteem.

Sense of Purpose | Young person reports that "my life has a purpose."

Positive View of Personal Future | Young person is optimistic about her or his personal future.

Chapter Eleven
Books on Denise's Personal Bookshelf:

Post Traumatic Slave Syndrome: America's Legacy of Enduring Injury and Healing by Joy Degruy Leary (Hardcover - Jan 2005).

What's Going on Down There?: Answers to Questions Boys Find Hard to Ask by Karen Gravelle, Nick Castro, Chava Castro, and Robert Leighton (Paperback - Oct 1, 1998).

Saving Our Sons by Marita Golden (Paperback - Dec 1, 1995).

RESTORING THE MALE IMAGE by Alex, O. Ellis (Hardcover - May 4, 2007).

Santa & Pete: A Novel Of Christmas Present And Past by Christopher Moore and Pamela Johnson (Hardcover - Nov 12, 1998).

What Mama Couldn't Tell Us About Love: Healing the Emotional Legacy of Racism by Celebrating Our Light by Brenda Richardson and Dr. Brenda Wade (Paperback - Jul 3, 2000).

Black Pain: It Just Looks Like We're Not Hurting by Terrie Williams(Hardcover - Jan 8, 2008).

MAMA KNOWS BEST: African-American Wives' Tales, Myths, and Remedies for Mothers and Mothers-to-be by Chrisena Coleman (Hardcover - May 11, 1997).

The Giving Tree 40th Anniversary Edition Book with CD by Shel Silverstein (Hardcover - Mar 30, 2004).

<u>What to Expect When You're Expecting:</u> 4th Edition by Heidi Murkoff and Sharon Mazel (Paperback - April 10, 2008).

<u>Sex for One: The Joy of Self loving</u> by Betty Dodson (Paperback - Mar 12, 1996).

<u>Act Like a Lady, Think Like a Man: What Men Really Think About Love, Relationships, Intimacy, and Commitment</u> by Steve Harvey and Denene Millner (Hardcover - Jan 27, 2009).

<u>A Woman's Worth</u> by Marianne Williamson (Paperback - Mar 8, 1994).

<u>Unfinished Business: Closing the Racial Achievement Gap in Our Schools</u> by Pedro A. Noguera and Jean Yonemura Wing (Paperback - Aug 18, 2008).

<u>A Piece of Cake: A Memoir</u> by Cupcake Brown (Paperback - April 10, 2007).

<u>Midnight: A Gangster Love</u> Story by Sister Souljah (Hardcover - Nov 4, 2008).

<u>In Praise of Prejudice: The Necessity of Preconceived Ideas</u> by Theodore Dalrymple (Hardcover - Sep 25, 2007)

<u>Race Matters</u>. Cornel West (Hardcover - May 25, 2001).

<u>Raising Kanye: Life Lessons from the Mother of a Hip-Hop Superstar</u> by Donda West, Karen Hunter, and Kanye West (Hardcover - May 8, 2007)

<u>Yesterday, I Cried : Celebrating the Lessons of Living and Loving</u> by Iyanla Vanzant (Mass Market Paperback - Aug 7, 2001).

Their Eyes Were Watching God by Zora Neale Hurston (Paperback - May 30, 2006).

Come On People: On the Path from Victims to Victors by Bill Cosby and Alvin F. Poussaint (Hardcover - Oct 9, 2007).

Sacred Pampering Principles: An African-AmericaWoman's Guide to Self-care and Inner Renewal by Debrena J. Gandy (Author).

Our Bodies, Ourselves: A New Edition for a New Era by Boston Women's Health Book Collective. Judy Norsigian (Paperback - April 19, 2005).

And on the Eighth Day She Rested: A Novel by J. D. Mason (Paperback - Mar 2003).

Girl, Get that Child Support by Cathy Middleton (Paperback - Oct 1, 2006).

What Every Woman Should Know About Divorce and Custody (Rev): Judges, Lawyers, and Therapists Share Winning Strategies on How to Keep the Kids, the Cash, and Your Sanity by J.D., Gayle Rosenwald Smith and Sally Abrahms (Paperback - Jul 3, 2007).

What Every Woman Should Know about Divorce and Custody by Gayle Rosenwald Smith (Paperback - Nov 1, 1998).

Chapter Twelve
Never Can Say Good-Bye

Black Woman to Woman

In my life I encounter many women and I am always amazed at the interesting stories women have, especially black women. Stories of childhood, relationships, and etcetera are always inspirational. I think I developed my love of women's stories from my maternal grandmother, Tena who spun stories better than any network ever could. From the time I could remember myself, every summer spent with her, Tena would sit by the kitchen window (after we all worked our asses off) and tell stories about life in a small southern town called McClellanville, South Carolina. These stories were certainly not age appropriate and discussed all matters from church, sex, relationships, life. The one constant component of every story from the many women I have listened to is: THEY NEVER GAVE UP.

These women who told me their stories also uphold other black women as well. I see too many black women putting down other black women in relationships, in public, everywhere, there is a certain level of disconnect with the majority of black women. Not all black women act this way, but I did say majority. We must show unity; greet and smile at one another. In business, if you got through the door, hold it open for another black woman to come through as well – don't feel threatened – encourage. We have become 'diva's' - too busy and too important to be kind, to be human.

I have witnessed black women in inter-racial relationships avoid black women in public. You children need to see you interacting with your people – which are their people. I have actually experienced first-hand young black girls stare me down like they can whip my ass when I walk into a school. Black woman to black women; allegiance, support, unity and respect are so vital and so very necessary.

What needs to be understood is not to envy what that black woman has; you do not know what she had to go through to get it. Instead of hatin' ask for some advice, you will be surprised at the support you will get. Black women must unify beyond the sororities, book clubs and churches. For the women who have it – pay it forward. **Remember – there are NO diva's in heaven!**

Saving a Black Son – Saving a Black Man

I have heard many lament about the lack of black men – it's time to stop criticizing and start supporting. Help a young black son – volunteer, mentor, donate, do whatever you can. Our black son's need us. There are so many programs focused on female empowerment, esteem building, educational support, and more. I certainly strongly agree there has to be support of girls and women, we cannot forget that the men of color – black men especially have been downtrodden and subdued as well as women in society. There is so little support for our young black sons. When the young son goes out into the world, it's tough. **Let's face it - young people DO have stress!** Successful parents understand this. To save a young black son is to save a black man. We have lost so many already to prison, drugs, violence, drop out, and the media induced hype. It is time to take our black men back – one black son at a time. Instead of saying: "I don't have time for _____" - make time.

Be strong in raising your black son – say NO, maintain boundaries, demonstrate and command respect. Work side by side, shoulder to shoulder with your black son, don't let go of your black son, don't assume that he has to 'man up' and you must let him be on his own = BIG MISTAKE!!! Your black son is still a child emotionally and mentally. He cannot begin to describe what is going on in his mind and body and you feel you must let him go? Hold onto your black son. This does not make him soft, or take away from his manhood – your child needs you to guide him and be a trusted, constant presence. Move away from societal expectations, forgive and move on. If a man has hurt you in your life, this does not mean that all men will hurt you. Black women, please stop blaming all black men for the transgressions of a few. This behavior is passed onto our black sons unconsciously. This is not all about you; your black son needs you *and you need him.* The unconditional love your black son gives is healing, inspiring and God sent to help you grow.

It is time to invest in the black son – the 400 years of slavery is over. Black women can now have their son's and love them and mother them forever. **Don't just breed your black son – be accountable for him.** Now that you are a mother – you are on a different level of womanhood and you must respect this level with maturity, accountability, sacrifice and **self control**.

Remember – Every black son saved is one less black man on a corner or in prison.

What does it take to be a successful black single mother: loyalty, accountability, trust, respect, boundaries, intellect, goals, sacrifice, forgiveness diligence, and self-value. All of these attributes make up a successful single black mother. She puts her black son first. Your black son motivates you to be the best woman you can be.

400 years of slavery has grossly impacted the black family including black motherhood. As slaves the black woman had to breed children in order to build the capital of the plantation. This was actually an early form of empowerment – America could not be what it is today if not for the black slave mother having babies. Black motherhood in America is **not** the same as motherhood in other races. Motherhood for black women is not seen as a form of empowerment; in fact the opposite occurs – entrapment, financial struggle, societal control, negative attention seeking, all of the attributes that were endured by the black slave mother – our black babies are now enduring today.

The new slavery is media driven; prison prosecuted, drug/alcohol addicted roles that make a profit off of blacks, but does not benefit blacks. It is time to take back our black men one black son at a time – it is time to embrace motherhood for what it truly is – empowering.

Black Woman – Find yourself; I often think of my mother telling me as a young girl who was raised in the south – she had to go out into the woods and 'find her religion.' I say for black women – FIND YOURSELF. You are not what the media tells you, you are not what the latest fashion label is, you are not complete by a man – Let God help you find yourself.

The world simply does not care if you don't care. The world owes you nothing. Do not abandon yourself or your black son. Sex is powerful and a woman who controls her sexuality is a powerful being. Be selective with sex and don't confuse lust with love. **Don't fall into the societal expectation that YOU MUST HAVE MORE CHILDREN!!!** I have been pressured for YEARS to have more children. People compliment me on what a good mother I am, and that I should have more babies. I did not take them up on the insistence. I am fully aware of my economical and social status and I did not grab onto a fantasy - it was and is a challenge raising one child and I never lost focus of that! DON'T LOOSE FOCUS!!!

I am one of you; I raised my son alone for 18 years. My two marriages were very brief. I grew up in a two parent home but my father was always working, so in essence my mother was a single parent. My father and I had quality time together – but it was my mom who handled everything else. Being the man my father was – there isn't a man in the world that could provide for me the way my father did: he did protect us, provide for us and made sure everyone knew that this was his family and he was very proud of us. In his own way – he was my father. My mother was on the front line and sometimes I knew society was brutal in stigmas but my parents held fast to their belief of the importance of family and education. I uphold those very same beliefs today.

Even with supportive parents, I chose the wrong men – twice – gave my egg to the wrong man – my son's father but it was the values taught to me by my parents that kept me focused on my son. My second marriage failed because I believed that my son needed a two parent home – **not true.** My son needs me – safe, with a peace of mind and goals to accomplish. **The black son can thrive and survive in a one parent home that is stable, safe and**

focused on the black son as opposed to living in a home of abuse, dysfunction and the focus not placed on the black son.

If you, the black mother are currently living in a home with the father of your son and there is dysfunction (alcohol, drugs, violence, dominance, indifference) and the focus is not on your black son – **DON'T LET YOUR BLACK SON GO!!!**

Here is what happens if you do: The black prince, your black son will learn how to cope within a dysfunctional home. Children are excellent at adapting – with a price. Your black prince will develop a coping skill, a way to deal within the dysfunction and once this black son becomes a man he will either avoid relationships, exhibit an inability to emote feelings or respond to partner in a relationship, date outside of his race as the result of resentment of you the black mother for not protecting your black son – this black man believes black women to be inadequate, your black son could develop sexual dysfunction towards women, your black son could become addicted to drugs/alcohol as a way of self medicating to mask his depression.

ANY OF THESE OUTCOMES DOES NOT MAKE A HEALTHY BLACK MAN OR A SOUND KING!

Have you ever seen a black man without emotions? He is flat in affect when it comes to any animation or feeling response. When his wife, sister, mother, daughter, friend tries to engage him, he is slow to respond if he responds at all, it is without feeling. He controls his diet and just about everything else in his life. This black man probably grew up having to adapt to suppress his emotions or 'man up' in order to survive in an environment of dysfunction or his defense mechanism kicked in for so long, now he does not know how to shut it off and demonstrate feelings. The black woman in turn faces a blank wall of silence when it comes to this black man demonstrating any emotions.

Black woman – find yourself – save your black son. There is an old southern saying: "When Mama Ain't Happy – the Whole House Ain't Happy!" The black woman is the foundation of the black family and if there are cracks or an inadequate foundation, the whole house falls. **There is no love greater than a mother's love both scientifically and spiritually. THAT is empowering!**

Black single mother, make a clear and sound investment in your black son. Don't buy him all the latest Jordan's and threads when his teeth are in need of dental care, his skin is a mess and he has no manners or respect. Don't buy your black son that hyped video game when he can't read or pass his classes. Do not pawn your black son off to the media hype! Invest wisely in your black son!

Black Single Mother – Stop Looking for Validation from Society.

Black single mom – you are not going to get your props, kudos, validation, apology or praise from society. You won't get it from your son's father, family court or the world for that matter – so stop looking for it. Your time of glory, validation, and appreciation comes through the achievements of your black son. The day my son graduated from high school over a year ago was something I cannot describe – I am still floating. I had a vision that day. God took me to a very high mountain top and we were so high in the sky, the sun was close and hot, everything was so bright. God showed me all the years of work with my son, the many mistakes I made, the growth, the laughter as well as the many achievements my son made and the people who cheered me on in this adventure called black single motherhood. God and I had a wonderful dialogue, I don't know for how long I had this vision but it was very through. I was offered closure, I was given a new life and God acknowledged my commitment to raising my prince. I realized that this was the only validation I need or want. I have my son's love, I have the knowledge that I am a successful black single mother – I am wealthy beyond measure.

I want you to have what I have – to experience the joy and growth that has led me to become an empowered black single mother. Black motherhood is not a travesty; it is a blessing and must be treated with sacrifice, seriousness and supreme faith. It is time to save our black sons from years of discard, disdain and discouragement.

Many single successful black mothers have come before me. I want this action to become mainstream and not sprinkled with a few exceptions. There is millions of Barak Obama's waiting to become kings. Imagine if Ann Dunham, Barak Obama's mother did not put her focus on her black son's education. Young Barak was home schooled <u>before</u> going to school every day. His knowledge became an esteem builder – working with his mother side by side, shoulder to shoulder saved his life. Education saves lives. Barak Obama's mother made that sacrifice of waking up at 4:30 AM every morning to teach her black son before he went to school. Sports was NOT the focal point, education was.

Save our black men – save our black sons. Black motherhood is not always pleasant, there will be rough days and times of uncertainty. Faith in yourself and the love of your son will sustain you. God is always there to pick you up whenever you fall, you won't have far to go.

Why did I use black son so many times? – To get my point across; the world views your son first by the color of his skin; then by his intellect. I hope this book is helpful to you and your black son the prince & future king.

I felt divinely driven to get this book out to women. I could not have been the successful single black mother that I am today if it were not for HIM.

I know you are tired and weary – but don't parent to keep the peace – parenting is not a peaceful act. Don't give in to your black son when you have already said no. Keeping the peace means blurring those boundaries and roles. Your black son sees you doing this, he will expect the world to do this as well and that is just not going to happen. Keep parenting and life transparent.

I want to apologize for any typos or errors you may find. I know I edited this book a million times...It was my goal in writing this book that the format remain simple as if a single black mother were right next to you – talking to you. I love black woman and this is my way of supporting you. Take back black motherhood – save our black sons.

My Web page in its growth stage! www.boldlioness.com.

Denise Bolds is a single parent by choice after two divorces. Her son, Jordan is now a college freshman. Ms. Bolds holds a Master's Degree in Social Work, with Medical Social Work being her specialty. Ms. Bolds is also a Community Activist and Advocate. Ms. Bolds is currently working on her second book: Learning to be Leaders: A Student's Guide to Successfully Completing High School.